Locked In

A Young Woman's Battle with Stroke

Locked In

A Young Woman's Battle with Stroke

Judy Mozersky

The Golden Dog Press
Ottawa – Canada – 1996

ISBN 0-919614-64-7 (paperback)

Canadian Cataloguing in Publication Data

Mozersky, Judy, 1970–
    Locked in : a young woman's battle with stroke

ISBN 0-919614-64-7

    1. Mozersky, Judy, 1970–Health.   2. Cerebrovascular disease–Patients–Biography.   I. Title.

RC388.5.M69 1996   362.1'9681'0092   C96-900730-2

Cover design: Gordon Creative Group.

Typesetting: Carleton Production Centre, Nepean.

Printed in Canada.

Distributed by:
    Oxford University Press Canada,
    70 Wynford Drive, DON MILLS, Ont., Canada, M3C 1J9.
    Phone: 416-441-2941   *   Fax: 416-444-0427

The Golden Dog Press wishes to express its appreciation to the Canada Council and the Ontario Arts Council for current and past support of its publishing programme.

To my family,
especially my wonderful parents

Epigraph

Monsieur Noirtier was seated in his wheelchair, in which he was placed in the morning and from which he was lifted at night. Sight and hearing were the only senses which, like two sparks, still animated that physical body already so close to the grave. As often happens when one organ is used to exclusion of others, in his eyes were concentrated all the energy, strength and intelligence which had formerly been distributed throughout his body and mind. He commanded with his eyes, he thanked with his eyes; and it was almost frightening to see them flashing with anger or sparkling with joy in that otherwise stony face. Only three persons were able to understand his language: Villefort, Valentine, and his old servant Barrois. But since Villefort saw his father only when absolutely necessary, all the old man's happiness lay in his granddaughter; and through devotion, patience and love, Valentine had come to be able to read all his thoughts in his eyes.

It had been arranged that the old man would express assent by closing his eyes, refusal by blinking them several times, and a desire for something by looking up at the ceiling. If he wanted to see Valentine, he would close his right eye only; if he wanted Barrois he would close his left eye.

Noirtier looked up at the ceiling, a sign that he wanted something.

"What do you want, grandfather?" asked Valentine. She began to recite the letters of the alphabet, stopping to watch his eyes at each letter. At N he signaled, "Yes."

"Ah, it begins with an N," said Valentine. "All right, is it Na? Ne? Ni? No?"

"Yes."

"It begins with No," said Valentine. "Good." She went over and took out a dictionary, opened it before Noirtier and began to run her finger up and down the columns. At the word "notary" he signaled her to stop.

"Is it a notary you want, grandfather?"

"Yes."

"Do you want me to send for one right away?"

"Yes."

"Is that all you want?"

"Yes."

"You have been sent for by Monsieur Noirtier de Villefort here," said Villefort after the first exchange of greetings with the notary. "His paralysis has deprived him of the use of his limbs and his voice. It's hard even for us to grasp a few scraps of his thoughts."

Noirtier appealed to Valentine with his eyes, an appeal so serious and imperative that she immediately said to the notary, "I understand everything my grandfather wishes to say . . . Monsieur Noirtier closes his eyes when he wishes to say 'yes' and blinks them several times when he wishes to say 'no,'" said Valentine. "And however difficult it may seem to you to discover his thoughts, I'll demonstrate it to you in such a way that you'll have no doubts on this subject."

from *The Count of Monte Cristo*,
by Alexander Dumas

Table of Contents

Foreword

This remarkable book tells a singular story—that of the experiences, feelings, and thoughts of a talented young woman whose totally aware and intelligent brain operates within a body that she can feel but can scarcely move in any way.

Suddenly, on a June day in 1990, Judy Mozersky developed the worst headache of her nineteen-year-old life. She had previously experienced severe migraine attacks complicated by neurologic symptoms but nothing like the bursting sensation she felt that day. Within minutes she found she could not walk. In the days immediately following, she lapsed in and out of conscious awareness, then reawakened only to find that she had totally lost her ability to move and to talk. Fortunately for Judy's future general health, her bodily sensation returned, as did her sense of smell and taste along with intelligent vision and ability to learn. Even today, however, although she has regained some crude voluntary neck movements, she can communicate only by blinking her eyes or moving them vertically so as to transmit coded verbal signals to comprehending friends, family, and caregivers. Otherwise, she quite literally lives locked in a body that in no way can express the movements and behaviors that enable most of the rest of us to stand, sit, move about, play, dance, talk, or meet personal needs.

Judy's reflections on the years since that catastrophic late spring day could easily have produced a harrowing tale of bitterness and plaintive self-pity. Instead, she proves a straightforward, remarkable analytic observer, as well as one almost devoid of self-indulgence. Despite all her suffering, she remains able to sense and empathize with the grief of others. In this dimension, she reminds me of some of the courageous young people I cared for over 40 years ago, who were severely paralyzed from throat to toes by poliomyelitis. Even though they were totally dependent on machines to breathe and sometimes could neither swallow nor speak, several of them learned to communicate by eye signals. Not all, but some of them possessed personalities like Judy's: always more sensitive to the troubles of and interested in the progress of other, similarly affected patients. Exposure to this kind of empathy among very ill persons can instill an enormous degree of humility in doctors and other caregivers; Judy Mozersky's book now offers a similar example of selfless optimism and motivation to a much larger audience.

Medically, what process could be so cruel as to produce Judy's plight? Briefly stated, despite her young age she suffered an acute stroke affecting the lower, non-thinking part of her brain called the brain stem. We use the term "stroke" to designate the injury that results when an artery that normally delivers oxygenated, nourished blood to a particular region of the brain's tissues becomes blocked. Unless the occlusion either quickly dissolves or becomes rapidly bypassed by adjacent blood vessels, brain tissue will die quickly — within a matter of a few minutes to a very few hours.

Judy's brain-stem stroke almost completely severed the downward traveling nerve-fiber pathways that normally connect the motor-executive areas in the higher brain, called the cerebrum, with the nerve-cell centers in the brain stem and spinal cord, which control the body's muscular movements. When this happened, Judy's conscious wishes and commands lost their capacity to direct any movements of her body other than those that partially regulate the muscles of her eyes, her throat, and her respiration. Automatic breathing, circulation, swallowing, digestion, maintenance of body temperature, and endocrine regulation remain intact but cannot be voluntarily changed. Judy's thinking, feeling, emoting, and intending brain remains unscathed.

What caused Judy's stroke? The immediate cause was a blockage of the large basilar artery, which lies at the base of the brain stem. What caused this blockage is uncertain. Most strokes result from processes caused by arteriosclerosis, high blood pressure (hypertension), or both. Given these predominant causes, strokes are far more common in persons older than age 60 years than they are in young persons. The smoking of tobacco and the taking of cocaine or amphetamine-like drugs sometimes cause acute strokes, but Judy had no such exposure. Certain rare immunological or inherited disease of arteries may cause strokes in young persons, but Judy showed no trace of such disorders. She did, however, carry two other stroke susceptibility risks. One was a history of what neurologists call complicated migraine; the other was the taking of oral contraceptives, widely called "the pill.'

Both migraine and acute stroke are relatively common illnesses. As such, chance alone might be expected to produce both disorders in a few persons. It appears, however, that the migraine trait produces a small but measurable independent risk factor for the development of stroke. This is especially true in young women like Judy, whose migraine attacks are preceded by visual scintillations, blind spots, or temporary weakness. As for oral contraceptives, current studies indicate that their use at least doubles the risk of young-age stroke. Accordingly, impression has it that the combination of migraine and oral contraceptives intensifies stroke risk.

As those who read this story will see, despite her devastating paralysis, Judy has lost neither her mental functioning nor her upbeat, young person's vibrant curiosity and focus on the future. Soon after recovering from the acute complications of her stroke, she learned how to express alphabetical language by an eye-blinking code. According to her companions, the result comes close to the speed of normal, everyday linguistic conversation. Her considerable intelligence remains intact. Since the onset of her stroke, she has successfully and competitively passed college courses necessary toward completion of her Cornell University degree. Through all this siege of illness, the essential Judy has not changed. She may have the physical limitations of an elderly person with stroke, but she retains the vivid enthusiasm and intelligence of a young woman. Her story provides an inspiration both to other stroke patients and to the doctors who care for them. It also stands as a tribute not only to the strength of her own character but to the awe-inspiring qualities of her parents, especially her imaginative, plucky mother.

The reader inevitably will ask, "If a person of any age had a stroke today, could it be treated more favorably than was Judy's in 1990?" One cannot be sure as yet, but there are promising preliminary signals coming from the use of new research-level drugs and other approaches now being tested in stroke victims. All these new agents will require prompt application and carefully supervised use if they are to become effective. Individuals experiencing acute stroke symptoms, such as sudden loss of memory or language or acute weakness of an arm or leg, should immediately go or be taken to a medical center that has a continuously available trained stroke team. Agents that may reduce the size of a stroke or open up the blocked artery that caused it are being widely tested. But time is of the essence and to be successful, most treatments must be started within two hours of the stroke's onset.

What of the future? Can persons with neurologic disability from stroke or brain or spinal cord injury realistically hope for scientific "breakthroughs" that will allow them voluntary movement of their presently paralyzed muscles? As yet, no such methods exist as a practical matter. Research in neuroscience and biologic engineering is moving at a fast pace, however, and a few promising beginnings already have appeared. Advances in computer science may allow us to develop complex but lightweight apparatus engineered to respond usefully to minimal stimuli from handicapped patients. One can envisage such equipment driving, for example, presently paralyzed arms, legs, or even voice boxes by means of codes emanating literally from the flick of an eyelid.

Taking a more biologic approach, one can envision future technologies that might bypass areas in the brain or spinal cord that have been damaged by stroke or injury. In most strokes and spinal injuries, brain areas that signal movement remain intact; the problem lies in the fact that the long, cable-like nervous tracks that connect the brain's directions to the final muscle innervating nerve cells of the brain stem or spinal cord are interrupted before ever reaching their target. Usually, the area of disconnection is relatively short and normal nerve pathways and muscle-moving nerve cells below remain functional. Some pioneering studies in experimental animals have already shown that such bypasses can restore the capacity of a severed optic nerve to carry visual signals to the brain. Other experiments offer hope that regenerating nerve fibers can be "teased through" the blocked area and reclaim the pathway to the still relatively normal bundles and nerve cells that lie downstream. Still other experimental work has shown that with proper nurturing, human nerve cells taken from patients receiving necessary brain surgery have the capacity to grow outside the body. The next step in such experiments will be animal research to determine if it is possible to put such cells back into the brain in order to replace those lost by stroke or injury.

These approaches indicate that Judy Mozersky and others with paralyzing injuries from stroke and trauma have reason to look hopefully to the future. Worldwide, many laboratories are attacking the barriers that presently limit regeneration or recovery in the brain or spinal cord following stroke or trauma. The future holds great promise, but scientific success will inevitably take time and can be made only if the public continues its presently high levels of support for medical research.

Beyond any doubt, Judy Mozersky will experience enormous satisfaction if she finds that telling her brutally graphic story of being locked-in has stimulated new medical research on the problem of stroke and has induced other potential victims of the disease to seek and to obtain rapid, effective treatment.

Fred Plum, M.D., Chairman
Department of Neurology and Neuroscience
Cornell University Medical College

Acknowledgements

Firstly, thank you to my wonderful family. My mother, my father and my brother, David. My family never stopped believing in me. Thank you to all the nurses who have cared for me since my stroke. Special thanks to Danielle Headrick, my tutor. Love and thanks to Karen Gardner who inspires me in everything I do. Thanks to Alexia, my editor and Jane, my agent. Thanks to all those who contributed to my book. My great appreciation to Dr. Nelson and Dr. Grinnell and Dr. Plum. Thanks especially to Jane Charlton who helps me with everything I do. Love and thanks to all my friends who have supported me from the beginning, especially Andrea and Giselle. Deepest love and gratitude to my dear grandparents who made all of this possible.

Judy Mozersky
Ottawa, 1996.

The Girl Who Could Not Move But Could Fly

Here is a little tale
About a girl whose luck ran stale

After high school she went to Cornell
She loved it there — her life was swell

But one day she became very sick
She had a condition no doctor could fix

She was unable to speak and unable to move
She was told her condition would never improve

Unfortunately it was no joke
This young girl had had a stroke

She became so very depressed
She would not eat nor would she get dressed

This went on for about a year
Her mind was filled with anger and fear

How is a kid supposed to live
When life has nothing more to give

Then one day she said, "No more sadness
I cannot blame everyone else for this madness

I cannot move and I cannot speak
But I can still imagine and think"

She imagined she was a normal kid
With legs that could dance and a voice that could sing

She imagined she could fly like a bird
Her mind took her all over the world

Her life now seemed to be so much fun
And she stopped being sad and was getting things done

She imagined she was an enchanted princess
With hair of silk and a golden dress

Her wheel chair was her gilded throne
It sat in her palace which was her home

All of her nurses were her maids
They fed her brownies and purple Koolaid

Because the girl could never speak she learned to talk in wise
    disguise
And learned to spell by using her eyes

In her palace everyone was the same
They all spelled with their eyes because their lips were lame

She imagined she was a free wild gazelle
With no splints or braces or problems to tell

She could dart through the forest or bask in the sun
She could scamper and jump and leap and run

She imagined she was a tiny butterfly
A soft whisper soaring through the sky

Her wings were spun of silver thread
The white fluffy clouds were her cozy bed

Wherever she landed such joy did she bring
She made children dance and got the birds to sing

For that young girl's mind let her be
Happy and normal and ever so free

So that was the lullaby
about the girl who could not move but could fly so high.

Judy Mozersky

Introduction

I lost everything in one night. Before this, I knew nothing of not moving or not speaking or not eating or not breathing. I was carefree and perfectly contented. Like my friends, I was only aware of good marks, parties that lasted all night and serious boyfriends. Like my friends, I was also taking birth control pills.

I remember the first time I was told what was wrong with me. A nurse in Intensive Care said to me, "You've had a brain-stem stroke. Worst one I ever saw. You have a condition called 'locked-in syndrome.'" You can't move or talk but you can think."

"I know," I said to myself.

ONE

"I lost everything in one night."

IT was the morning of Thursday, June 14, 1990. I was nineteen years old and a junior in college. My home was in Ottawa, Canada, but I was at Cornell University taking a summer course. I was a psychology major and was using the summer to finish the statistics course required for my major.

I had just gotten out of the shower when I heard the phone ringing. "I'll get it," I shouted to Julie, my roommate. I would pass the empty bedroom with the phone on the way to my room. As I was about to answer the noisy telephone, I felt something burst in my head and got very dizzy.

"Julie, Julie," I screamed, "I'm going to faint. Call Gannett. I know the number."

Gannett was the medical clinic at Cornell. I knew the phone number because I had visited the Center for various minor ailments over the past two years.

Julie called. She explained what had happened and they told her to bring me right over. "And now my left side doesn't work," I cried to Julie. She told Gannett and they repeated their advice. Julie hung up and said hurriedly to me, "Let's get you dressed and over to Gannett."

Julie was in my sorority. We had also been roommates that year and knew each other quite well. We were taking a summer course in statistics and sharing a lofty apartment above a yogurt shop. I must have trusted Julie completely because from that moment on I let her take care of me.

I hobbled into my bedroom. Julie threw some sweats on my towel-clad body and pushed me out my door. "I can't walk," I cried hysterically. "I'll carry you," Julie responded just as hysterically. After this, I can't remember clearly. I'll try to describe the events that followed as accurately as possible.

We somehow made it to Julie's car and then to Gannett. We were waiting for the elevator at Gannett when I said, "Julie, I'm going to throw up. Hold my hair." Julie passed me a garbage can and proceeded to get my long wet slippery hair out of my face. I proceeded to vomit.

Just then a nurse appeared with a wheelchair. I embraced the sight of it gratefully for I really could not walk. I somehow ended up on the examining table upstairs. The doctor was a stern-looking female. "I always say that women with migraines shouldn't take birth control pills," she told me when she learned of my history. "So, what is wrong with me?" I asked impatiently, ". . . a mild stroke?"

"I doubt it. You're much too young," she replied.

"So what is wrong with me?" I repeated, still impatient.

"Probably just a migraine. Quite a severe one, mind you, but we'll send you to the hospital just to be safe," the doctor said calmly. "Julie, hold my hair," I ordered again, "I have to throw up."

I somehow got to the hospital. I think I woke up once in the ambulance on the way there. A male attendant was leaning over me. I was lying on a stretcher. "I have to throw up," I told him. And I did.

I do not remember arriving at the hospital nor do I remember Julie's arrival. I found myself in a little room in which Julie was standing nervously.

"Your CT scan showed nothing. Isn't that a relief?" Julie asked.

"Yes," I replied. "So, what is wrong with me?"

I started to cry again. "It is four o'clock," Julie told me. "You have been throwing up all day."

"How pleasant," I commented sarcastically. "We missed our exam, Julie," I suddenly recalled.

❖

"Call my parents," I told Julie a little later. "I need them. Call John." Maybe tomorrow isn't the best day for him to visit, I reflected. John was my boyfriend at the time. Unbeknownst to my parents, he was supposed to be visiting me the next day. At that point, I still believed I'd be fine. I could still partially move and talk.

A doctor then walked into the room. He looked like a hippie, with long, dark brown hair. He immediately saw that I was throwing up in my own hair and he tied my hair back with an elastic. "I know how to do this," he explained. Another doctor entered the room. This one had short red curly hair. "I'm Dr. Vaillancourt," he said.

We did not know then that he was to be the primary physician involved in my stroke while I was in Ithaca. We did not even know I was having a stroke. We did not yet know that the pill had caused my stroke. We did not yet know that my migraine headaches put me at risk for a stroke once I was on the pill. Dr. Vaillancourt then started to chat and told me that he too was from Canada. I started to throw up. Dr. Vaillancourt examined me. He asked me to stretch out both arms. The left one wavered and fell.

"My left side just does not work," I told him matter-of-factly. "And now I see double and my lips are numb." I was crying again, not from pain but from fear and dread. A few strands of hair had come loose and were soggy and wet. I choked on them because they were in my mouth.

"Hmmm," Dr. Vaillancourt paused, "You definitely have a neurologic problem."

"You don't know what's wrong with me?" I asked accusingly.

"Probably just a bad migraine. But I'd like to watch you in the hospital," he replied and left the room soon after.

My memory is blank as to how I spent the early evening. Julie went home. I was transferred from Emergency to Observation, where I was to spend the night. I did not know that I would wake up in the Intensive Care Unit.

Apparently I had a conversation with a nurse at around eight o'clock at night and had been very coherent and lucid. Also, I finally stopped throwing up. I have no recollection of that evening until about midnight when I heard my mother say, "Hi, sweetie. Mommy and Daddy are here." I was so relieved. They would make this ridiculous migraine better. Dr. Vaillancourt was there, too. He was wearing shorts and asking me to do things.

"Point your foot," he commanded. He was holding my left foot. I tried with all my might but I just couldn't. My mother turned to my father and said, "She is so bright and hard-working." "I still am," I wanted to tell her. I wanted to comfort and reassure her but I couldn't.

I couldn't move.

I couldn't speak.

I'm not sure what happened next. My condition overwhelmed and completely bewildered me. I remember having another CT scan. I remember a beige band being wrapped around my head. It pulled my hair. When it came off, Dr. Vaillancourt decided to cut my hair free from the band. I didn't even care. Dr. Vaillancourt did some more things to the back of my arm.

Suddenly I heard another voice say to my mother, "It's two o'clock in the morning. Now is when we lose most people."

"I can hear you," I wanted to scream. "I hear and understand everything. How dare you talk about me as though I can't hear you?"

But, of course, they didn't know that. And I certainly couldn't tell them.

❖

Julie G: Judy and I had shared a room with our friend Lauren in our sorority house during our sophomore year, and Judy and I had grown close. A statistics course was required for psychology majors, and since I was a psychology major, too, Judy suggested that we both stay in Ithaca at the end of the year to take the course during the summer. We didn't know many other people in Ithaca, and we spent the majority of our free time together.

I was more uptight about the workload and the requirements of the course than Judy and tended to get stressed out over the material we had to cover. Judy, on the other hand, knew that the work had to be done and realized that neither anxiety nor intimidation would get the assignments done effectively. She frequently reminded me to put the class in perspective: It was summertime, after all, and this one course was not ultimately going to determine my future.

That Thursday, Judy and I decided to go out for a relaxing lunch before the exam. But we never did make it to lunch. Judy called me as she was getting out of the shower, saying that she felt extremely dizzy. I tried to help her out of the bathroom and into her bedroom so she could lie down, but as I moved her down the hallway she started having problems speaking. She was slurring her speech, and I had trouble understanding her. She said she felt really sick. One side of her body went limp. She said, nearly inaudibly, that no matter how hard she tried she could not control her speech or limpness.

As I described Judy's symptoms to the Health Center over the phone, I realized that they were characteristic of stroke victims. But I do not have an M.D. after my name and whatever limited knowledge I had of stroke symptoms always related to experiences of the elderly. I decided I must be crazy to think such thoughts, that Judy was just having another of her migraines — although this migraine was the worst I'd ever seen Judy experience. When I hung up the phone, I knew that we couldn't wait for the Health Center to send someone to pick us up. Judy's speech was still slurred, but I somehow realized that she was trying to say, "My condition is getting worse."

I had to get Judy dressed quickly. She was basically helpless, limp in my arms. After getting her dressed, I put her arm around my neck and dragged her with me down the hallway, down the elevator, and down the street to my car. My parking spot was relatively close to our apartment, but that day the trip to it seemed endless.

At first, they would not let me keep Judy company at the hospital because I was not family, but I somehow managed to talk myself to her bedside. I was pretty scared for Judy, but I tried to keep her mind occupied by talking about anything removed from the day's events. I know that this was ten times more difficult for Judy than for me, especially since nurses repeatedly entered to take tests or give Judy medication. I asked Judy if I should call her parents, but we both concluded that it was not going to be necessary, so why scare them? Judy kept slurring out something to the effect that we were going to miss our afternoon statistics exam. Now it was me telling Judy to put things into perspective; I promised that I would contact the professor and get the matter taken care of. Later, I did call her parents.

Judy's father: The first phone call came from the neurologist attending Judy, Dr. Vaillancourt. I had just arrived home; Anne was at a dinner meeting of her school committee. Dr. Vaillancourt introduced himself and said that Judy was in the Tompkins Community Hospital. She had suffered what appeared to be a severe migraine earlier that day, and he was going to keep her overnight for observation. He said that she seemed to be recovering, and there wasn't any strong reason for us to come down to Ithaca.

I called Anne and told her about Dr. Vaillancourt's call; she said she would come right home. About an hour after the first call, Judy's roommate, Julie, phoned from Ithaca. While she said that Judy appeared to be OK, her headache earlier in the day had been "really scary." Those two words were ominous. We had already decided to go to Ithaca.

We made arrangements for our thirteen-year-old son, David, to stay overnight with a friend from school. We told him that Judy was hospitalized with a migraine and that we would be away for a day or two.

We left Ottawa around seven p.m., having packed for an overnight trip. We were nervous all the way down, but we couldn't have prepared ourselves for what confronted us when we arrived in Ithaca five hours later. Judy was not able to communicate with us. She had been placed in a pediatric ward for observation. The nurse told us that she had been lucid, but about an hour or so earlier she had started to get "floppy." Dr. Vaillancourt arrived shortly thereafter. He took Judy for CT scans. We helped to move Judy onto the gurney and wheeled her through hospital corridors.

There was no movement from Judy, who was running a fever at this point. Dr. Vaillancourt said he had to rule out brain diseases such as meningitis and encephalitis as the cause. At around three or four in the morning, Judy was moved to Intensive Care. There was a small waiting room nearby.

We didn't yet know exactly what was wrong. We did know that Judy was very sick. I remember Anne wondering aloud how much of our little girl we were going to get back.

The staff at the hospital were very comforting. They placed a cot and some sheets and pillows in the ICU waiting room so we could get some rest. The next day, they offered us a hospital room, which we gratefully accepted. We did not know that we would be spending a week there.

TWO

"I still couldn't move or speak."

I'D always wondered if people in comas can hear. Unfortunately, I found out. They don't hear or remember anything. I really don't know how long I was in a coma because time had lost all meaning for me. It was probably between twenty-four and thirty-six hours.

While I was comatose, Dr. Vaillancourt performed a whole battery of tests. He was still trying to determine what had happened to me. So were my parents. So were my friends. Julie visited me the entire time I was comatose. She also brought a friend of ours named Alison.

When I woke up, I was in Intensive Care. I still couldn't move or speak. Actually, I couldn't communicate at all. There must have been a flight pathway right behind the hospital because I kept hearing planes landing nearby. My grandparents were also there. They are very devoted and I wasn't at all surprised to see them. I don't think I realized how ill I was.

One of my clearest memories is of my mother establishing a communication system with me shortly after I came out of my coma. I would look up when I meant yes and down when I meant no. This was vital — and a great relief. Even though I couldn't talk, this simple system gave me some freedom and some ability to make decisions. It worked very well provided that my partner asked the appropriate questions.

I had a very high fever and very vivid dreams all week. I dreamt that I was transferred to another part of the hospital, which was outside. I was in an Intensive Care Unit along the seashore. Each room was a breezy pink tent and the bed stood on pale beige sand. I had another dream that John and I were going to a store to buy wooden forks, and one in which Julie was helping me put on earrings. This dream felt so real that a few months later I thought I was still wearing the earrings. I was later told that those dreams were in fact hallucinations. At any rate, they were most odd.

I have another friend also named Julie. She is not from my sorority; I know her because she lived on my floor freshman year. We had plans to go out to dinner Monday evening. I was of course in no shape to go out. I still believed I 'd be fine, that I was just having a ridiculous migraine. Anyway, Julie came to visit me at the hospital. I could tell that she was shocked by my appearance. I was surrounded by tubing and i.v. poles and machinery. She talked for about an hour. My parents were with her. "Look, Judes, Julie is here," my mom pointed out excitedly. "Julie is here," my father repeated, as though her visit had some curative power.

I wanted so desperately to tell Julie that although I looked decidedly foreign amidst all those needles and tubes, I was still the same Judy, her Judums.

A lot of people came and called that week. I guess that bad news travels fast. Still, no one knew precisely what was wrong.

With most strokes there is some cognitive damage—loss of memory or the ability to understand speech or recognize familiar objects or people, or general disorientation. I certainly was not aware of any. At one point my father tried to determine exactly how much cognitive damage had been done. He was wearing a blue shirt. He asked if his shirt was green. I looked down for no. He asked me if his shirt was red. I said no. He asked me if his shirt was blue. I indicated that it was.

He got all excited and told Dr. Vaillancourt. "Hmmm," Dr. Vaillancourt said. He still didn't know exactly what was wrong with me.

My grandfather is a very wise man. And I know that he talked to me a lot during that first week. I was practically deaf, though, from the swelling in my brain, and I missed most of what he was saying.

On Tuesday, my roommate Julie told me I'd had a very complicated migraine. "I'll say!" I thought and agreed with her. That day, I had an MRI, which stands for Magnetic Resonance Imaging, a very sensitive test that takes a detailed picture of the brain. It showed Dr. Vaillancourt that I had definitely had a stroke. My father elaborated: "You are cognitively perfect," he explained. "Now, your motor functioning is another story. Some nerves have been severed forever, some nerves will rejoin, and some nerves must be rerouted to their endings. Dr. Vaillancourt is cautiously optimistic."

My father sounded relieved. I still didn't know the full extent of my sickness. All I knew was my present condition. My Uncle Danny had come down from Ottawa, so I knew I was very ill. Much later my mother reflected that they had been very nice to us in Ithaca. This was because this was the worst thing they had ever seen.

❖

Julie G: At seven on Friday morning, I had a phone call from Judy's parents. They told me that things had taken a turn for the worse during the previous evening. I didn't really understand what they meant, but asked when I could see Judy. When I arrived at the hospital, they told me that Judy was in Intensive Care and was no longer conscious. Something had happened during the night. Mrs. Mozersky told me that I should just talk to Judy and keep her company. Although I wasn't sure Judy could hear me — she was just lying there, hooked up to more machines than I'd ever seen in one room — I talked to her about anything and everything. She seemed so helpless. Yesterday she had been having difficulty moving and speaking, but this — what was this???

Judy's mother: Judy awoke the next day, but couldn't make a sound. Nor could she look straight at us or move her eyes from side to side. While Judy was in the coma, her eyes had had a weird colour and flatness. When she came out of her coma on Saturday morning, her eyes suddenly looked quite different — they were the old Judy eyes. Even though they weren't moving normally, they were back to their usual colour. They looked bright to us, and alert. We desperately wanted to know if she was aware of what was happening. We couldn't determine if Judy had cognitive damage without being able to communicate with her. So we decided to ask Judy some questions and tried to establish that when she looked up, the answer would be "yes" and when she looked down, it would be "no."

Judy's father: Judy was comatose for twenty-four to thirty-six hours. It was probably Friday afternoon or Saturday morning when we became aware of the nature of her condition. She'd had a stroke, although we wouldn't know until the doctors had seen an MRI of her brain exactly what damage had been done.

Dr. Vaillancourt asked us if we knew that Judy was taking oral contraceptives. We hadn't. Judy had asked him on Thursday not to tell her parents that she was taking birth control pills. When he told us, it at least offered some explanation for her stroke. No other cause seemed plausible.

Judy's mother: We had been told that Judy would probably have trouble with her memory and so we set up little tests to see what she remembered. I had some magazines and would show her a photo of, say, a dog. I would then ask, "Is this a flower?" No. "Is this a car?" No. "Is this a dog?" Yes!!! We did this with several items and colours and Judy's answers were always accurate. We talked to her all the time, telling her where she was, what was going on, where we were going, and so on, as if she were able to understand everything. On Sunday Judy's boyfriend John was coming up to see Judy and she let Ken know that she didn't want to see him. "That's great," commented my mother, who had come up to Ithaca with my father to be with us. "She remembers who he is." We just kept trying to determine what she could remember. While we were in Ithaca, a speech pathologist suggested the idea of a spelling system. We didn't begin to work it out until Ottawa, relying on "yes" and "no" answers through that first week.

Judy's parents: By the time we left Ithaca, we knew that Judy had suffered a stroke in the brain stem, the part of the brain that acts as a highway for messages traveling between the brain and the spinal cord and controls such basic functions as breathing We also knew there was some swelling in the brain from the stroke and that we wouldn't have the full picture until about three months later, after the swelling had subsided. We clung to this information with great hope. Dr. Vaillancourt was very helpful and let us see the MRI films and explained what we were looking at and where the damage was.

Judy was in pretty fragile shape. Because she wasn't able to swallow, her mouth was propped open so saliva could be suctioned. She couldn't bear being flat on her back because she felt like she was choking. She had a naso-gastric tube leading to her stomach so that she could get nourishment. She had a urinary catheter. Her feet started to "drop" very soon after the stroke and we were advised to get high-top running shoes to put on her feet to keep them at a ninety-degree angle so that her Achilles tendons wouldn't shorten. Her body would spasm and her arms would become rigidly straight and turn inward. She had no control over her facial muscles. Most upsetting was the flatness of her facial expression—no affect, no smile, no expression at all. It was jarring and upsetting. Her eyes *could move only up or down, not sideways. Her jaw was extremely rigid and we couldn't get her to relax her mouth and open it. She would grind her teeth uncontrollably. It was terrifying.*

THREE

"Even my skin hurt."

I flew from Ithaca to Ottawa on Thursday, June 21. I was supposed to leave Wednesday night but I was in no shape to fly. I was to travel with my mother. "I've always wanted to ride in a helicopter," she said, "only not like this." "Me neither," I thought. We flew to Ottawa in a small air ambulance plane instead.

I was so uncomfortable that even my skin hurt. It felt like daggers were searing my eyes. I had various tubes coming out of my mouth. I had a catheter, of course, but I wasn't even aware of it until weeks later. My fever was so high at that point that I wasn't aware of much. I was attached to some machine by my left arm, but I don't know what the machine was, or what other machines I was attached to. I was truly grotesque. There were also some nurses on the airplane. My mother kept asking me if I was all right. I responded yes because I had no way of conveying my discomfort. The plane ricocheted all over. I was so scared that we would crash.

When we arrived in Ottawa, it was raining. An attendant shielded me from the rain with a black umbrella. I was taken to the Ottawa General Hospital. I was to stay in Neuro-Observation, which is a mini-intensive care unit for brain and spinal cord injuries. It was a large pink room. There were eight beds separated by pink curtains. A nursing station was located in the center of the room.

I was brought to a side room. My Uncle Dan was there waiting with my Aunt Joy. "I have a headache," Dan complained. "Don't worry, Judy. Not a migraine," my uncle, who does in fact suffer from migraines, reassured me. I guess one stroke per family is enough.

Two nurses helped transfer me from the stretcher to my new bed. It was a special bed called a Clinitron. It was a big air mattress that prevented bedsores. One of the nurses helping me was male. I didn't know yet that I would hate male nurses.

At dusk, a tall, older man with sandy brown hair approached me. "Hi," said the man. "I'm Dr. Nelson."

"Good," I thought. "I need you, as you can see. I've had a terrible stroke."

Naturally, Dr. Nelson knew I could hear, although not very well, and understand everything. I could even communicate. I did this by spelling with eye blinks, even though everyone except my parents was too intimidated to spell with me.

I'd been told of Dr. Nelson. He was one of the finest neurologists. "Dr. Nelson!" a nurse had exclaimed earlier. "Oh, you are in great hands."

"And I need them," I thought.

Dr. Nelson was a kind, gentle, fatherly man. He never chastised me for taking birth control pills when they made my migraines worse. He never chastised me at all. I appreciated that.

I had many tests while I was in Neuro-Observation. One of the first tests I had was a test of cognition. My speech therapist was a bald male named Marc. He determined that I could spell and he made me a laminated alphabet board. My parents had already concluded that I could spell. They were using a makeshift spelling chart made of coloured paper. I didn't spell much, however. I was too sick.

By evening I didn't remember any particular test. Being the neurotic psychology major that I am, I spelled out "multiple per-sonality" to my parents, since one of its symptoms is loss of memory.

I had developed a terrible habit since my stroke: I constantly had my mouth clenched shut so that I ground my teeth. The noise drove my nurses and my family and Dr. Nelson crazy. I am pleased to say that that behaviour ceased after a while.

The nurses in Neuro-Obs were excellent. They were, on the whole, the best nurses I ever had. One nurse in Neuro-Obs was especially nice. Her name was Dale. I still keep in touch with her. She was a perky blonde with wide blue eyes. She had a new baby named Danielle about whom she talked incessantly. I adored her.

There was one rough nurse assigned to me. I dreaded her arrival in the morning. She treated me like a regular patient. "Doesn't she know my skin hurts?" I thought. "Hasn't she ever handled a stroke patient before?" I didn't yet know how rare brain-stem strokes were. I didn't know I was the youngest brain-stem stroke Neuro-Observation had ever seen. I didn't know most stroke patients can't feel anything.

My Aunt Joy and Uncle Dan lived very close to the hospital. My parents went to their house every night for dinner before returning to see me, after spending all day with me.

I was lonely but I had a horrible time dealing with the thought of any friends visiting me. I knew they wouldn't be able to understand me. That, unfortunately, foreshadowed much of my future. People would inevitably have a difficult time understanding me. I was too sick for visitors. My friends couldn't handle this. I couldn't handle this.

Finally, however, my loneliness outweighed my apprehension. I decided to see my friend Andrea. She and I had been friends since we were babies and she probably knew me better than anyone in the world. I knew she wouldn't care how sickly I looked. She would just be relieved that I was alive.

Andrea came on a Sunday. She was wearing a small print flow-ered shirt and faded jeans. She smelled like French fries. I looked at my own tube-feeding with disgust and wondered enviously when she had eaten.

I cried when I saw her. "She always does that when she gets emotional," my mother explained to Andrea. She knew this because on the night I returned to Ottawa my little brother, David, came to see me. I cried when I saw him. He cried, too. He had obviously not been adequately prepared for the shocking transformation I had undergone. My mother had taught David to communicate with me, but I still somehow sensed that he feared me.

When Andrea came, she talked quite a bit, but my left ear was still deaf so I couldn't hear her. As I knew it would, Andrea's visit saddened me. "How totally preposterous that I've had a stroke," I thought, bitterly. I knew that none of my friends must endure this. They were probably lying in the sun right now tanning their stomachs. Had I not taken ill, I too would have been wearing jeans and eating fries. Instead, I was wearing a night gown and subsisting on a liquid diet fed to me through a tube in my nose. I looked wonderful!

I got very sick a few days later. My parents were going to David's eighth-grade graduation and not coming to see me. I spiked a high temperature and I started to breathe horribly.

"Her mom says she breathes funny when she gets anxious. But why would she be anxious?" I heard one nurse ask another.

"Because her parents didn't come tonight," the other nurse replied.

"I think I'll call Dr. Nelson," the first nurse said.

I guess she called Dr. Nelson, and my parents as well. Dr. Nelson arrived within minutes. I do not think he expected me to get so ill because he had sent me to Neuro-Obs in Ottawa from Intensive Care in Ithaca instead of straight to Intensive Care. He listened to my chest. "Hmmm," he said, "I don't think it's just anxiety." I was most upset. I certainly couldn't get any sicker, but sicker I did get.

"Tomorrow we're going to put a small tube in your neck," said Dr. Nelson.

Just then my parents entered the room. "Hi, sweetie," exclaimed my mother. She was dressed in fuchsia. She looked nice. "Can I talk to you alone for a minute?" Dr. Nelson asked my parents. All three of them left the room. I was left with a nurse. When they returned, Dr. Nelson said to me, "Judy, we are sending you to Intensive Care."

❖

Judy's parents: To communicate with Judy, we spelled with her. In the beginning, we divided the alphabet into two halves. We'd ask if the letter Judy wanted was in section 1 or 2. Then we would tediously go through all the letters until her eyes went up. We quickly refined the system by dividing the alphabet into four parts, determining which quadrant contained the letter, and then going through the six or seven letters to get the right one.

Dr. Nelson: What is commonly called a "stroke" occurs when an area of brain tissue is deprived of blood supply and oxygen for a significant period of time. This is usually the result of a blockage of a blood vessel, most often by a blood clot, although this can also occur if a blood vessel becomes constricted or goes into spasm. In this case, a blood clot may form secondarily in the narrowed blood vessel. Most instances of brain damage due to a blocked blood vessel occur suddenly and it is this more or less sudden loss of function that we call a "stroke." The focal area of brain damage will cause specific symptoms related to the particular area involved. For instance, if the area of the brain which controls arm movement is damaged, the person will have a paralyzed arm. It is not uncommon for one entire side of the body to be affected.

In Judy's case, a major blood vessel at the base of the brain — the basilar artery — became blocked and the adjacent areas of the brain were permanently damaged. These areas, which are known collectively as the brain stem, are those which conduct nerve impulses from the motor part of the brain (from which voluntary movement arises) down into the spinal cord and out to the muscles of the limbs. In addition, when there is damage to the brain stem, nerve impulses cannot reach the face or vocal apparatus. Thus Judy has lost the power to voluntarily control her face, speech, arms or legs. The centers which control her eye movements are located higher up in the brain stem and thus escaped damage. Judy's vision and hearing were also spared because of the location of their pathways.

Because of the location of the blockage and its severity, Judy's stroke affected much more of her body than a stroke that occurs elsewhere in the brain and typically affects speech or hearing or one or more limb, often on the same side of the body, but does not leave the patient totally paralyzed.

I had been alerted by Dr. Vaillancourt as to Judy's medical condition before she arrived. She was sedated and I am rather surprised that she subsequently had so much recall of events associated with her trip to Ottawa. We often do not realize that people in a locked-in state can in fact see and hear normally and Judy was obviously capable of doing both. She had no mental impairment and she and her parents had already established a method of communicating by using the movements of her eyes. Usually we have to teach patients such methods and it takes a while for both patients and caregivers to learn it. I remember her mainly as appearing at that time as a terribly frightened young woman. It was hard to reassure her that everything was going to be all right and yet be honest with her. I knew she could not be deceived by half-truths. This was a girl for whom it was clear that honesty was most important.

Cognitive processes usually reside in the "grey matter" or cortex of the cerebral hemispheres. Judy certainly has no evidence of any cognitive impairment and this is as would be expected in that all of her brain damage is in the brain stem, the part of the brain that handles such "automatic" functions as breathing and swallowing and also serves as a conduit for the messages from the cerebral hemispheres or thinking, willing part of the brain to the muscles of the face and limbs.

At this point, Judy was still very sick. She was having uncontrollable spasms of her jaw muscles and we brought a dentist in to see her about this as we were afraid she might break her teeth. She had to be given muscle-relaxing medication and eventually this resolved. Brain-stem strokes are uncommon, but not really rare, accounting for some 20% of cases in older people. They are, however, much less common in younger patients.

Many patients have sensory disturbance after a stroke. In some cases, there is complete loss of sensation, but in others there is a distortion or perversion of sensation, as Judy experienced. This is fairly common in brain-stem strokes.

Judy's brother: When I was in grades five, six, and seven, Judy and I were as close as a brother and sister could be, especially where there's six years between them. Then Judy went away to university, and we started to grow apart. As I think about it, I'm probably lucky that she went away to school, because if she'd had her stroke while she was still my best friend in the whole world, it would have been a lot harder to deal with. As it was, I missed her a lot, but I was only twelve or thirteen, so I lived with it without too much difficulty.

When my parents got the phone call from Ithaca saying that Judy was in the hospital, I had about two weeks of junior high left. My parents assured me that everything was fine and arranged for me to stay with a friend; they told me they'd be back in two or three days. They called every night and told me they'd be a little longer than they had expected.

A week later they flew Judy back to Ottawa in an air ambulance. I still didn't know that she had had a stroke; my parents must have had a lot on their minds and they either forgot to tell me or didn't want to worry me.

I went to see Judy in the hospital the first day she was back. When I got there, my Uncle Danny took me for a walk around the hospital to tell me what had happened to Judy, since I still didn't know. He told me what had happened, what to expect, what she looked like — everything. I remember crying while listening to him.

When they finally let me in to see Judy, I wasn't ready for her. She was in a room filled with other people I didn't even notice until I left. I walked over to her bed and sat down beside her. I don't know *how long I was there, but all I did was hold her hand and cry. We both cried.*

Andrea H: *Judy and I have been best of friends for many years. After my first year away at school, I was looking forward to spending some quality time with Judy. Judy was still at Cornell finishing off a summer course when I got home, but I knew she would be home soon.*

On June 16, a mutual friend of Judy and mine called me at home. He was very confused and tried to explain a conversation he had had with Judy's roommate. What he was describing to me was a bit hard to follow, but I did understand one thing, the word "stroke." I was stunned. I decided to phone Judy's uncle and aunt to see if they could clarify the story I had just heard. To my disbelief, they confirmed everything that my friend had said.

I didn't quite know what to do. Judy was my best friend, and I felt helpless. After what seemed like forever, Judy's parents finally called me. They told me that Judy wasn't ready to see anybody at the present time. I told them to send her my love. I knew all I could do was wait until she was ready to see me.

A little time passed and Judy decided she was ready. I went to visit on a Sunday afternoon. I picked up her brother David and we went to the hospital together. He had obviously already spent time with Judy, so he tried to prepare me for the visit. When I got to the Neuro-Observation Unit, Judy's parents were waiting to greet me. We talked for a short while in the waiting room and then proceeded to Judy's room. I kept telling myself I was going to be strong, but nothing could hold back my tears when I finally saw her. Judy began crying, too, which made it very difficult for me. I didn't quite know what to say. I remember thinking, "Do I say, 'I'm sorry'? Do I ask how she's feeling?" I was at a loss. I started talking about the things I had been up to over the past few weeks, but everything seemed so trivial. "Why would she want to hear about my life?" I kept thinking to myself. But since I did not yet know how to communicate with Judy, it was all I could do. I was simply happy and relieved that she was in Ottawa and that I could finally spend some time with her.

FOUR

"I always felt like a freak and on display."

INTENSIVE Care was a frenetic blur of whirring, buzzing, and ringing. ICU is the place where the sickest human beings are kept alive by machinery operated by healthy human beings.

A nurse named Peggy greeted me. "Hi," she chirped brightly. "Welcome to Intensive Care." I was in no mood for chirping nurses. My parents left me in the hands of Peggy in a small white room. I thought of my friends and missed them. Then I went to sleep.

When I awoke I was hooked to a number of monitors. I was still having trouble breathing. The next day they put that "little tube" in my neck. The tube in my neck was called a tracheostomy tube. It stung and was extremely painful.

The doctor who performed the surgery was blond and wore glasses. "We gave her enough anesthetic to knock out a horse," he told my mother. "She'll be asleep for twenty-four hours."

"Oh, good," responded my mother. "She needs her rest."

I didn't know then that I would have my trache for the next four months. "We want to do away with those tubes in your mouth," announced Dr. Nelson one day. "We'll have to put you on a respirator."

I was too sick to react. I was desperately unhappy in ICU. I felt abandoned and drained. Nobody understood how I needed to go home. I hated ICU and I longed for the security of my house. I cried constantly, every day. When I woke up in the morning and saw the respiratory therapist fixing my respirator, I cried. When my Aunt Joy came to visit every morning, I cried. "Do you want to spell?" she would always ask, knowing perfectly well that I did. "Yes," I would always respond.

My first message was usually about wanting to go home. "Just to sleep," I would beg her. "I can just sleep at home." My Aunt Joy always explained why it wasn't feasible or realistic for me to go home.

One day my Uncle Dan explained all the steps through which I'd have to pass before I could sleep at home. "You are still in ICU," he reminded me. "After ICU you'll go to Neuro-Observation for a while. Then you'll go out on a regular ward for a while. Then you'll go to Rehabilitation. After that, you can go home." "How incredibly depressing," I thought to myself.

I was ready to go home now. Every night I would cry to my parents, "Get me out of here." I would plead, "Don't leave me here." I cried to my nurses all day. I think it bothered them.

One nurse was particularly kind. Her name was Caroline and she spoke French . She had long brown hair and was pregnant. She was mostly my nurse at night. Once she told me about the trees outside the hospital. "Maybe one day you will look out a window and see the trees, " she told me. "Well, it certainly won't be in ICU." I thought. There were no windows in ICU. "Most of our patients are unconscious," Caroline had explained, "So it doesn't matter if they don't have windows."

"But what about your patients who are conscious?" I wanted to ask.

"Maybe, just maybe, one day you will actually go outside and see the trees for yourself," Caroline told me. "Of course I will," I thought. I never for one moment doubted that I would get better. Everyone else obviously thought I would die.

Fortunately, friends weren't allowed to visit in Intensive Care. I was at a point where I wanted nothing to do with them. My mother would bring in their letters every morning after the mail came. I was so miserable that at first I wouldn't even let her open the envelopes. I did not want to hear about their tans or their boyfriends. I was completely stunned at my position. I stared at the hose connected to my tracheostomy and felt completely alone. My only hope was that my parents would see how desperate I was and bring me home. But they didn't.

One day I needed to have my hair washed. It had not been washed since I'd been in Neuro-Obs. My cousin Lolly came over to help wash my hair in bed. My mother was very concerned that we dry my hair thoroughly.

"She already has pneumonia," my mother explained to Lolly. "Nurse, look what I brought." My mother held out a small blue fan. There were so many machines in ICU that we couldn't plug in anything like a fan to blow dry my hair. The small fan was battery-operated. Lolly and my mother spent many hours drying my hair. When they had finished they braided it so it wouldn't be a bother.

Because there were no windows in ICU there was no day or night. It was in ICU that I lost my excellent sleeping ability. To this day I still need sleeping pills to get to sleep.

I had a private room but all I could see and hear were machines. There were no flowers allowed in ICU. The walls were plastered with cards from my friends, which of course I could not read. The lights were fluorescent and they made an oppressive atmosphere in the crowded room. I needed a window.

Every morning a group of doctors and medical residents made rounds. I hated the noisy group that gawked at how rare a specimen I was. I always felt like a freak and a display. The residents were particularly close to my age. They would spell with me. I wanted to tell them how dreadful a place was ICU, that I really didn't belong there, but nobody would have listened.

After one of these rounds a nurse named Nancy stared at me. I was, of course, crying. "I have some good news for you," she chirped." "Good," I thought. "I could use some."

She drew in a breath. "Neuro-Observation wants you now."

❖

Judy's parents: A week after returning to Ottawa, Judy developed breathing problems. At this point she was transferred to Intensive Care to have a tube put down her throat — to be intubated — so her breathing could be helped with a respirator. Several days later, still in ICU, she developed pneumonia. Our understanding was that the swelling in her brain stem was affecting her breathing center, and that once the swelling subsided and the pneumonia went away, she would resume breathing on her own. We were told that the pneumonia was a predictable result of Judy's being paralyzed and unable to swallow.

About a week after going into ICU she was given a tracheostomy — a breathing tube was placed directly in her trachea. It was an inflatable trache, which meant that a balloon around the outside of the trache tube would keep saliva from moving into her lung. This was necessary because Judy's pneumonia was most likely the result of her aspirating some saliva into her lungs. With a trache, however, Judy would need periodic suctioning to clear secretions from her trachea. It was hard to watch this being done and difficult for Judy to put up with. She had that trache for almost four months.

Judy's mother: In ICU Judy was attached to many machines and they all made noise. The noise factor and the lack of natural sunlight made the whole place very nerve-racking. Judy was afraid to be left alone, without a family member at her side, so we worked out shifts.

Judy was seen by everyone: neurologists, respiratory therapists, physiotherapists, speech pathologists, residents, and medical students. To help the nurses communicate with Judy, we wrote out lists of questions that she could answer with a "yes" or "no." For example, "Are you cold?" At this point, we were still trying to see what parts of her body she could move. Every morning we'd ask, "Can you squeeze my finger?" No. "Can you move your foot?" No. Judy's mouth was still closed tightly and we were working on helping her relax and try to open it.

Every day there were X-rays of her chest. She had a heart monitor, and every day her blood gases were monitored as well. An arterial tube was put in her arm so they wouldn't have to insert a needle each time blood was taken. Judy had always hated even the thought of needles and suddenly she was being given needles for everything. I remember watching one day as they drew blood from her arm; when it didn't move at all while they were doing it, it really hit me that Judy was paralyzed. I had never thought about what the word really meant until then.

Judy's parents: One of the things that kept us hopeful in the early stages was the unusual nature of Judy's stroke. A brain-stem stroke in a young person is rare and most of the information we had about brain-stem strokes — Ken's brother Dan was reading up on the condition in the medical school library — seemed to pertain to more elderly people who had prior histories of high blood pressure or circulation problems. We couldn't imagine that Judy's youth and spirit weren't going to work in her favor in this case. She had so much energy and determination, she had survived the kind of stroke that often kills people, and we were sure she would just do better than anyone imagined.

We kept waiting for a sign that things were going to improve. We clung to calendar hopes. We were told that the first thirty days were critical; then six weeks became a possible marker for a breakthrough; and then finally, knowing it was a long shot, we hoped that some recovery would possibly be detected after three months. As we were coping, we would say each night, "Well, maybe tomorrow there will be a big breakthrough." That attitude kept us going — but Judy never had the big breakthrough we were hoping for.

Judy's optimism was typical of her basically positive nature. None of us could really believe that things could get worse, or at any rate, wouldn't improve. And even in Intensive Care, Judy remained very much Judy. For instance, when friends suggested the healing possibilities of various kinds of sounds, we got hold of a number of "new wave" tapes of forest sounds, babbling brooks, ocean waves crashing on the beach, bird chirping, and soft, soothing piano music. But Judy immediately spelled out "CHEZ," the call letters of an Ottawa rock radio station that had always been her favorite. She wasn't interested in any of the other tapes we had obtained for her. And CHEZ remains her constant radio choice even today.

Judy's frustration with ICU was understandable and we felt as powerless as she did. We knew the chaotic nature of the setting was upsetting and the ever-changing tide of nurses was overwhelming, so we just tried to be there with Judy as much as possible.

We didn't have a real prognosis until about three weeks after the stroke, when we had a visit from Dr. Fred Plum of the Cornell Medical School. He is a neurologist who has had a lot of experience with brain-stem strokes and coined the term "locked-in syndrome." He came to Ottawa with Judy's grandfather while Judy was in ICU and was probably at her worst.

Dr. Plum was straightforward and grim in his description of the situation: Judy was very, very ill. Further, he said she was very depressed and he recommended that she begin taking anti-depressants as soon as possible. He did not see the possibility of much improvement and cautioned us that we would have some very tough decisions ahead of us.

Anne had stated beforehand that if he gave us a dismal prognosis, she would simply not believe it. However, it was very hard to shake this off. How were we ever going to help her make a life for herself, and how were we ever going to get on with our lives? We were devastated.

As far as Judy dying in ICU — we didn't know what to expect. We didn't really believe it would happen, but we knew that if Judy were to have another major event of any kind — stroke or respiratory failure — the outcome and damage would be uncertain. We knew we were being prepared for all eventualities, but we could only believe she would get out of ICU and go back to Neuro-Obs, which we were recalling with greater and greater fondness. It became a goal.

Judy's father: We were still perfecting our communication with Judy and hadn't yet learned of the perils of trying to guess what she was spelling. One day in ICU she had her hair washed, then done up in a certain way. She kept spelling "B-R-A-I . . . " and we kept finishing for her, ". . . brain, Judy, is your brain hurting?" fearing that this poor child was dying of brain pain. After several false starts, Judy finally got it out: "My braid kills! Move my head so I don't lie on top of my braid!"

Dr. Nelson: Judy had developed pneumonia, and we presume that it was due to aspiration. Pneumonia is not a common accompaniment of most strokes, although aspiration pneumonia occurs frequently in patients who have brain-stem strokes because they have weak respirations and have difficulty coughing and usually have difficulty swallowing. Because Judy had weak respiratory movements, we had to insert a tracheostomy tube into her windpipe and assist her respirations for a short time by putting her on a respirator. Patients with brain-stem strokes often develop damage to the respiratory center and stop breathing. This is the most common cause of death in these people, and we put Judy on the respirator in case her spontaneous breathing should stop. Fortunately we were able to carry her through this period and her respirations became stronger again. Eventually we were able to discontinue the respirator and remove the tracheostomy tube.

In the Intensive Care Unit patients usually have difficulty sleeping because of the twenty-four-hours-a-day noise and bustle. Also, sleep-waking patterns are organized in the upper brain stem, and people with brain-stem damage very often have disturbed sleep patterns. Loss of sleep can lead to depression, and depressed people often have disturbed sleep patterns, but depression can also be associated with damage to the brain stem.

FIVE

"I had my first hospital birthday."

I started to cry when I got to Neuro-Observation. "She always cries when she gets emotional," my mother explained to the puzzled nurse.

I was very happy to return to Neuro-Obs. I didn't know why I was being transferred other than that I knew I must be improving. I welcomed the pink warmth of the sixth floor graciously. I welcomed all the nurses. I even welcomed the sound of the man in the bed next to mine, who moaned every time he exhaled.

I had a nurse I remembered and liked very much. Her name was Susan. The first thing she did was remove the electrodes from my chest. "Yay!" I thought. No more heart monitor. I was off a respirator. I was off all machines. I still had a feeding tube, but no machines.

Around this time I developed a bladder infection from my catheter. To my shock and horror they removed my catheter and made me wear a diaper. I almost died. Diapers at my age! What would my friends think? But my friends understood perfectly. I didn't always have a nurse with me so I had to wear diapers.

The head nursing supervisor on the Neurology floor was a wonderfully kind woman named Hazel. She behaved just the way a head nurse should. She was always out of her office mingling with the patients and their families. Hazel spoiled me for future head nurses. She truly worked in the patients' best interest. She visited all the patients every day. I thought this was usual behaviour for a head nurse and came to expect it.

There is a branch of the Body Shop in Ottawa. I was forever using and smelling like its products and this continued in the hospital. I got my nurses from Neuro-Obs hooked on a particular scent called "Dewberry."

"Whenever I smell 'Dewberry,' I think of you," one nurse told me.

"Whenever I set foot in that store, I'm reminded of Judy," another nurse said.

I was extremely dependent on my parents. They had both taken time off work and were at the hospital from morning until night every day. They were terribly grieved by what had happened to me and I think were still quite shocked. Every evening they would push me in my wheelchair for a walk outside. One night I was with my father when he saw a man he knew.

"What happened?" the man asked as he walked over toward us.

"A stroke," my father replied, "in the brain stem."

"A stroke!!" exclaimed the man, astounded. "Brain stem? Do you mean the spinal cord?" he asked.

"No, the brain stem," explained my father, "located just above the spinal cord at the base of the brain."

"Wow!" said the man with disbelief.

I was still nervous about having my friends visit. My friends had always been and remained the most important thing in my life. But now that I was out of ICU, I wasn't as concerned about mere survival and I could think about them.

I decided to visit with my friend Lisa. Like Andrea, she had known me for many years. She made a book and a tape for me. As it turned out, it was not really difficult to see her. She quickly adapted to the fact that I couldn't speak and learned my alphabet chart.

My parents and I had devised a spelling system of communication using eye blinks. The alphabet was divided into four sections or quadrants. My spelling partner would name the four quadrants — one, two, three, and four. I would look up for "yes" when my partner named the quadrant that I wanted.

The first quadrant contained the letters "A" through "F." The second quadrant contained the letters "G" through "M." The third quadrant contained the letters "N" through "S." The fourth quadrant contained the letters "T" through "Z." My partner would then name each letter in the chosen quadrant. I would raise my eyes when my partner named the letter that I wanted. In this way I spelled words and sentences.

1	A	B	C	
	D	E	F	
2	G	H	I	
	J	K	L	M
3	N	O	P	
	Q	R	S	
4	T	U	V	
	W	X	Y	Z

I still didn't want to see my Cornell friends. I don't know why. I suppose I didn't want to be reminded of what I had been only a few weeks before — active, independent, carefree.

Every morning when I awoke I surveyed my body for changes. The most noticeable difference was an annoying tingling sensation in my arms and legs and hands and feet. This lasted for several weeks. Dr. Nelson was away on vacation so I told the doctor left in charge of me. He didn't know what it meant. I later decided it was sensation returning.

❖

The neurologist who had visited me in ICU had predicted I would get very depressed. He prescribed an antidepressant called Prozac. In Neuro-Obs they discovered that it caused sleeplessness. Dr. Nelson took me off antidepressants right away. To everyone's surprise I never became clinically depressed.

In Neuro-Obs I started having a sitter at night. I needed a sitter to stay with me because I couldn't call a nurse if I had another stroke or had difficulty breathing or needed my position changed. I became very scared at night. My parents found a sweet sixteen-year-old who sat with me through the night. Her name was Wendy. She had an older sister who was a nurse on the Neurology floor. I would later have her sister for a nurse.

At this point I was still being fed though a tube in my nose. Dr. Nelson and some other doctors kept asking me if they could put a tube in my stomach permanently. I kept refusing, thinking they would just have to remove it once I began to eat again.

I had been told that I would always need a feeding tube. I had been told that I would never eat again. I was truly horrified by that thought.

After a while, though, I consented to the surgery. A year later, I had my stomach tube removed.

I had my first hospital birthday that July thirty-first. It was very dismal and depressing. One of my nurses had the same birthday. She was turning twenty-five. I was turning twenty. I despondently wondered where and how I'd spend my twenty-fifth birthday.

I was in Neuro-Obs for almost four months. Most people usually stay there for about a week. When they leave, they go to "The Floor." The Floor was the ward outside of Neuro-Obs. Everyone talked about the Floor as if it were some magical and unknown foreign place.

One day my father was feeding me ice chips and I was sort of eating them. A nurse saw us and called the speech therapist who had been working on my swallowing. He came up and watched me eat.

"Hmmmm" he pondered.

A few minutes later the nurse returned. "Guess what, Judy? We're sending you to the Floor on Monday."

❖

Judy's parents: Fortunately, our employers were understanding about this family crisis and extremely generous about giving us time off. This was our routine: we would appear in Neuro-Obs in the morning. We would catch up on the morning's events and then one of us would go for lunch while the other stayed with Judy.

The most appalling and worrying part of Judy's condition was her total helplessness. She could do absolutely nothing for herself. We were her interpreters and we felt we had to be there at all times to help her. How else were people going to know the person who was locked in that motionless body? How would they know what Judy liked and didn't? We had to tell all the nurses and therapists everything Judy liked and liked to do. We had to make her as real and vibrant to them as possible.

We went through the daily torture of seeing how Judy's helplessness led to misunderstandings. At dinner time we would leave Judy alone in Neuro-Obs with the TV turned on to an acceptable program and her head propped so she could see the screen. Many times we would return an hour and a half later to find her head flopped down and the TV tuned to something ridiculous for her, like a show on swimming. It would absolutely kill us to see how helpless she was, forced to endure such irritating situations for quite some time. The nurses weren't negligent, but at dinnertime they were understaffed while they took turns going to dinner themselves. Although they would watch Judy through the glass window of her room, they had many other patients to attend to.

After dinner we would stay at the hospital until 9:00 or 9:30 before heading home. Our schedule was single-minded through that whole summer. Our son, David, was away at camp for six weeks, which was probably wonderful for him. And it gave us the freedom to spend time at the hospital without neglecting this wonderful fourteen-year-old.

Judy's brother: At the beginning of July, I went away to camp for six weeks. Of all the things I've ever done, I think that was one of the smartest. I don't know how I would have handled the situation with Judy if I had been stuck in the city all summer. But even though I was surrounded by friends at camp, with nothing to remind me of home, I still had a hard time. I remember having to find a counselor in the middle of the night once because I couldn't stop crying. That night was basically just a release for all the emotions I had been holding in since Judy's stroke.

Lisa T: I had known Judy for almost twenty-one years. We have been "best friends" for most of those years. When I found out that Judy had had a stroke, about a week after it happened, it was one of the worst days of my life.

I had no idea, really, of what to expect when I got to the hospital. One thing I knew about Judy was that she never sat still. She was always traveling: to Europe, to the States, or to Israel with me. And she liked to experience different things, from ballet dancing to partying at school to getting involved with theater.

To my surprise, the Judy I saw at the General Hospital that day in July was not the same one I have just described. Although Judy was cognitively able to understand everything that was going on around her, I was not cognitively able to understand the situation that presented itself to me at that moment. I was glad that Judy's cousin Lolly was on hand when I came to visit for the first time because I honestly don't know what I would have said to her on my own.

Judy was crying when I saw her for the first time. I felt like crying so badly but I tried to control myself because I didn't want to upset her further. The tubes and wires that surrounded Judy were very foreign to me. I could hardly believe that this was the same person I'd known for years and had seen only a few months previously.

Luckily, I pulled myself together and tried to communicate with Judes using the spelling board that the Mozerskys made up for her. Lolly was very helpful in lightening up the serious mood that we were in. We talked about school and life in general and I hoped that my being there was helping Judy to feel better.

Dr. Nelson: Brain-stem strokes often cause a loss of ability to swallow. Initially we put a small tube through the nose down into the stomach and feed the patient that way. However, this gets very irritating and can actually cause damage to the tissues in the nose and throat after a time. We then decide that a tube inserted directly through the abdominal wall into the stomach or small intestine is preferable. It is well tolerated by patients and avoids the danger of aspiration of food into the lungs as well. It was almost a year later that Judy recovered her ability to swallow and we were able to remove the tube. I was a little surprised but many stroke patients eventually regain their ability to swallow.

Judy's parents: Judy's feeding tube was not a big deal for us, but it was for her. At that point, Judy was still hopeful that the stroke would prove a short-term inconvenience in her life and that she would eventually be back to her old self. In that eventuality, having a scar from a stomach tube was not what she wanted. In the meantime, however, Judy had the not-so-lovely appearance of a person with a tube hanging out of her nose! Our biggest objection to the naso-gastric tube was that it frequently became dislodged and then Judy's feeding would be halted for a day or so until it was replaced correctly by a doctor. Each time that happened, Judy would come down with another infection. She had already lost a great deal of weight and she needed her nourishment to build herself up again and regain her overall health. Once the feeding tube was placed in her stomach, it was never visible, and without the nasal tube, she looked much more normal.

Judy's brother: I ended up coming home to visit for Judy's birthday halfway through the summer. It was tough to see Judy, who was always a very active person, lying so still in a hospital bed. Fortunately, I returned to camp the next day, where I could pretend I didn't have a problem in the world. All my friends at camp were really understanding and made things as easy as possible for me.

Judy's parents: Toward the end of July, about six weeks after Judy had had her stroke and was still in Neuro-Obs, there was a family

conference with us and all of the people responsible for Judy's care —
doctors, nurses, physio and speech therapists, and social workers.
We understood that we were to discuss goals for Judy. We went into
the meeting thinking about lofty goals pertaining to recovery and
discharge — when Judy would start moving, when they planned
to transfer her to the Rehabilitation Centre, what they thought she
might eventually be able to accomplish on her own. In short, we
were still in something of a state of shock and disbelief about her
condition and prognosis.

What we heard during that meeting left us depressed. The goals
that Judy's health care workers discussed — which had to do with
her most basic life functions, like breathing, swallowing, and freeing
her from life-support systems — were so far below what we wanted
to hear and gave us so little reason for looking forward to fuller
recovery.

We left the meeting in a daze, but shortly thereafter, we decided
to continue to work on our goal, which was to get Judy out of the
General Hospital and accepted into the Rehab Centre.

SIX

"It became increasingly clear that I was not typical of most strokes."

THE Floor was a letdown. I, of course, cried when I got there. Nobody questioned this. Fortunately, I only stayed on the floor for a little more than a month.

For the first time in my hospitalization I had a roommate. Her name was Gertrude. She was an elderly lady who had had a stroke. Stroke wasn't her only problem. Gertrude had various tubes in her chest to drain fluid. I knew this because she would call the nurses all day. They ignored her or sometimes came into the room just to appease her. "Now, Gertie," they would say condescendingly, " you are just fine."

One day my mother observed, "That poor woman is just terrified. She just wants someone to stay with her." I knew how she felt. I felt so totally alone and I had tons more company than Gertrude. I think she was comforted by my having a night sitter. A friend of Dale's had started sitting with me at night. Her name was Pam and she knew Dale from Newfoundland. I was still awfully frightened at night. Gertrude was too. She would call out to my sitter instead of ringing for a nurse.

An interesting assortment of characters lived on the Floor. There was Mr. Burns, who always wore a baseball cap and hollered down the hall. There was Leo, who had Alzheimer's disease and wandered into other patients' rooms and their belongings. There was Mr. Troy, who had had two strokes and who muttered to himself in garbled tongue. I was by far the youngest. Most of the others had also had strokes but they weren't sick enough to remain in Neuro-Observation and were too sick for rehabilitation. This meant that there was no hope of some stroke patients ever returning to live in the community. They would always have to live in some kind of institution. I would look around myself in amazement and ponder with incredulity that I now belonged there.

I think one of the saddest human positions is with the head lowered. So many inhabitants of the Floor had their heads lowered. They were waiting to be fed or waiting to go to bed or something. They looked dejected and pitiful and pathetic. I couldn't hold up my head either but people were always pushing it back for me. I would later work on holding up my head with a physiotherapist. Meanwhile the occupational therapists invented a method to hold my head back. They tied my ponytail to the back of my wheelchair.

A typical day on the Floor went like this: I woke up very early, sometimes to watch the sun rise. This usually occurred because my sleeping medication had worn off. On the floor my bed was right near a window. I could look outside and watch the leaves change colour. My room was directly across from the nurses' station because I still couldn't ring the call bell.

At seven a.m. someone would arrive to present herself as my nurse for the day. "Good morning, Judy," she would chirp. I would look up because I couldn't chirp back. She would wash and dress me. At ten o'clock I had occupational therapy, which consisted of things like adapting to a wheelchair and using foot and hand splints. I was supposed to be getting a switch for a call bell, but I never did. The only valuable aspect of O.T. was that it enabled me to make a social visit away from my room. At eleven o'clock I had speech therapy, where we worked on relaxing my mouth and helping me to swallow. At one o'clock I had physiotherapy, where we worked on range of motion exercises to keep my muscles from getting too tight from lack of use. I was free and bored after that. I often had a reader come in over the dinner hour to read me the newspaper and keep me company. My family usually visited me at night and we'd go outside for a walk.

I remember the first time I went outdoors. It was raining and my grandparents were visiting. It had now been almost three months since my stroke. I thought I'd get a mysterious or a prickly feeling from being outside after so long inside but I felt nothing special. It was nice but not spectacular.

I was so bored most of the day. I had a small TV but I never really enjoyed watching it. I missed Neuro-Obs. I really missed Dale. She sometimes visited me at night with her friend Pam. We would discuss cute doctors, of which I had none. I never became especially close to any nurses on the Floor. Maybe I wasn't there long enough.

I got very thin in the hospital. I had always been thin but never scrawny. My system simply could not adjust to a liquid diet. I finally stabilized on a feeding called Jevity. It was very rich. One nurse told me each feeding contained the equivalent of twelve cream puffs.

I had to work very hard to have my trache removed. I had to convince everyone that I was swallowing properly. I could even eat with a trache because I didn't aspirate food into my lungs. I told my dad and Uncle Dan: "Even test my swallowing." Finally, the doctors did test my swallowing. I passed.

A few days later, I had my trache removed.

My skin still hurt. The tingling had ceased, but I still hated to be touched. I especially hated to be touched on my hands. I don't think this is typical of most strokes, but it became increasingly clear that I was not typical of most strokes.

One day I had a nurse from Neuro-Obs. Her name was Joan. While she was washing my face she said thoughtfully, "One day you will write a book and tell all of us how it feels."

"I certainly will," I thought madly. "But it can't be like this." I was still communicating through eye blinks. I assumed Rehab would find me a computer but Rehab never found me a workable computer. And I spelled out an entire book with eye blinks.

Finally, after I'd spent four months in the hospital, a doctor from Rehab named Dr. Grinnell came to visit me. She had curly auburn hair. She asked me if I was ready to come to Rehab. I responded with an emphatic YES! My mother was there to interpret this.

"Good," said Dr. Grinnell. "I'll see you on Tuesday."

❖

Judy's parents: The Ottawa General Hospital is part of a medical complex that has a nice park-like area with a pathway running through it. We would take Judy in a wheelchair for walks outside and through this lovely sylvan area as often as we could. Before we went for these walks, Judy would have to be hoisted with a Hoyer lift from her bed to the wheelchair. A sling was placed under her, then attached to the lift; then she was lifted out of bed and into the chair — a production that involved several nurses and took anywhere from five to eight minutes. It wasn't until Rehab that Judy was treated to a two-person transfer.

On our walks, we would also take Judy to the cafeteria in the hospital, where we were eating more meals than we were eating at home. She would sit and watch us eat. As her condition improved, we would give her little tastes of smooth, easy-to-swallow foods, like ice cream or frozen yogurt.

We were very unsure where Judy would be going from the hospital. To get into the Rehab Centre next to the hospital became a goal and a dream. Rehab was connected to the General Hospital by tunnels inside and the surrounding paths outside, and our evening walks often took us there. We did not know if Judy would even be accepted by the Rehab Centre. Nonetheless, we would walk through it and talk about the day Judy might go there. Judy would quip about the eighty-year-old roommates she would have when she got to Rehab.

After Judy had moved onto the Floor, she was visited by several doctors who told her that she would be able to go to Rehab if she could remain free from infections for six weeks. We were elated! Everyone at the hospital told us how busy Judy would be with all her therapies at Rehab and how wonderful they were at making miracles happen.

Before Judy could go, she wanted to get rid of her trache. The doctors had to be certain that Judy could swallow before they would allow her to eat and to have her trache removed. That too became a goal. Judy had always been very goal-oriented. She was now finding herself locked in, with a different set of goals.

Before Judy could get rid of the trache, she had to build up her respiratory strength. This was part of her physiotherapy, and it proceeded in steps. The physiotherapist would place a tube with an opening over the opening in Judy's trache tube. By regulating the size of the opening, one could regulate how hard it was for Judy to breathe — how much effort it took to inhale and exhale. At first, the opening was large, but over time — and this took weeks — the opening was made smaller, requiring more effort from Judy to breathe. To make sure that Judy was getting enough oxygen, a clamp was attached to one of her fingers to read the percentage of oxygen she was transmitting to her blood. If it fell below a certain point — say, 85% — the opening would be enlarged to let more in and ease *her effort. Judy would do this for 15–20 minutes every day until she could sustain her breathing with the tube at its smallest opening.*

Before allowing Judy to get rid of the trache, the doctors also had to be certain that she was swallowing well and wouldn't accidentally aspirate her saliva. Judy kept telling us that she was swallowing just fine, but she first needed to have a swallowing test, which was arranged by the speech pathologist. We went down to a special room in the hospital basement where a very gruff radiologist took x-ray movies of Judy swallowing a radioactive liquid. The doctor and several people from the speech department carefully examined the films and pronounced Judy ready to have her trache "corked." This meant they plugged the opening, forcing Judy to breathe through her nose and mouth. Originally, they were going to cork Judy for just a few hours at a time to gradually build up her normal breathing. However, once the cork went in, there was no looking back for Judy. She did beautifully, and a day or so later, they were able to remove the entire trache tube. Within a day or so of its removal, the opening in her neck and trachea was beginning to close.

The departure from the hospital, although only a short walk away from Rehab, was emotional and dramatic for all of the staff and the family. The hospital staff had been part of our existence. One of the nurses told us that Judy would probably never be able to sustain herself by eating and would always need some tube feeding. Another goal!

SEVEN

*"Aren't you embarrassed to be seen with
me?"*

My first two weeks in Rehab were completely empty. My rehabilitation schedule hadn't yet begun. I had no occupational therapy, no physio, no speech therapy, no psychological counseling, and no recreational therapy. On the Floor, the nurses were always telling me, "When you get to Rehab, you will be so busy." They were so wrong. "Everyone in Rehab tells us how busy it is." I don't know what they meant. I was used to being an active college student and I couldn't imagine being busy in a hospital.

My parents visited me a lot. I shared a room with three other patients. My roommates were usually elderly, but I was getting used to this. The roommates I had in Rehab were often highly inappropriate. I once had a roommate who was blind. Since I communicate by blinking my eyes, we couldn't converse. Another of my roommates was so senile that she told my mother that I spoke when no one else was around. Imagine that!

My first occupational therapist was a French-speaking lady named Rachelle. She was pregnant and stayed only a short time. She was pleasant and efficient. My first physio was named Sue. When we first met, she was told that I didn't like the word "stroke." We decided to call it "my condition." She was a funny and personable brunette. I looked forward to seeing her because of her witty sense of humour.

I had previously told my mother not to tell people I'd had a stroke. I preferred that she say I'd had encephalitis or meningitis, two highly contagious brain diseases. Like Sue, she refused. I was ashamed in a way of having had a stroke. Strokes were not a concern of teenagers. Strokes were for crotchety elderly people, not young and sprightly ones like me. I should have been at Cornell taking psychology and dance classes. Instead, I was lying motionless in a rehabilitation hospital after a totally devastating stroke. I was a statistical oddity and I hated it intensely.

I hated when people spoke loudly to me as though I were deaf. I liked when people talked to me as though I were a normal individual, not a freak.

The first thing I did in physio was to continue the tilt board, an activity I'd begun at the General Hospital. I was literally strapped to a board and tilted upright. This felt refreshing and wonderful after lying down for so long. I also continued range of motion exercises. Sue knew how boring this was for me but she had to do it anyway.

My speech therapist was a dear woman also named Sue. She was slender and had light brown hair, and she dressed vividly. She had a son who was the same age as my little brother. Sue worked with me on trying to eat. She also had the joyous task of finding me a computer to communicate with.

I started on a computer that had rows of pictures instead of words. I had pictures of all my friends put on the computer. The switch to operate it was usually on my eyes. The process was frustrating and very slow. For example, Sue would point to a picture of my friend Kelly and say, "Stop on Kelly." I would blink my eyes when the light was on Kelly. This was my first computer. Later I would have one that worked from my flexing my trapezius muscle, one of the few muscles that I could contract consistently. But communicating this way was terribly tedious—even slower than spelling via eye blinks. This was my first letter:

HI KELLY

YOU GET TO BE THE FIRST

TO RECEIVE A LETTER WRIT

TEN BY MY SHOULDER.

UNFORTUNATELY THIS IS NO

T FASTER THAN MY EYES.

YOU KNOW HOW MUCH I LOVE

COMPUTERS

I HEARD THE NEWS ABOUT A.T. . . .

THIS LETTER TOOK ME A WE
EK TO WRITE.
LOVE JUDY.

Recreational therapy allowed me to write letters to my friends. I loved this. I also loved my therapists; we inevitably became fast friends. In addition, the recreation department sponsored various outings. I enjoyed myself on these because my mother went with me and talked to me. I didn't interact with the other patients, however, because I couldn't communicate with them.

Luc was my social worker. He had broken his neck at age nineteen and said I reminded him a lot of himself. His role was not particularly salient at the beginning of my stay in Rehab, but it became very important around discharge-planning time. Then he was my key to freedom, and I depended on him heavily.

At that time, my discharge planning was a huge unknown. I didn't know of any other person in Canada with locked-in syndrome who lived outside a hospital, but my parents were determined that I would have a good future. Working with Luc, they had to convince the authorities that I could live independently in the community. We didn't know then that the whole process would take nineteen months.

In Rehab I had primary nurses. This meant that whenever my assigned primary nurse was working, I had her as my nurse that day rather than just taking the luck of the draw. My first and most favorite primary nurse was Marilyn. She was a tall brunette. Her looks were always changing so it is impossible to describe her more accurately. Marilyn was the best nurse I ever had. She used her common sense instead of blindly following rules. If, for example, I was upset during a meal and Marilyn saw me, she would never make me finish eating or drinking. She would take me back to my room and spell with me and find out what was wrong.

Unfortunately, not all of the nurses were like Marilyn. Many of them did not take the time to spell with me, which meant that I couldn't communicate. I can't possibly convey how frustrating and infuriating this was. One would think that in a hospital the nurses at least would all learn how to spell with me. What a myth! Often at night, I would lie in my bed terrified and sobbing because I couldn't sleep. I would think terrible thoughts like "What if I have a migraine?" or "What if I have another stroke?" Nobody would know. I was afraid of dying and yet I yearned for the sweet release of death.

I would sometimes sob until a sympathetic roommate heard me crying and called a nurse. Seldom could the nurse who answered the call spell with me. So she would try to guess my problem. I usually told her that my arm or leg hurt because I was too angry to keep her guessing all night. Thoroughly traumatized and upset, I would lie awake the rest of the night.

Sue, my speech therapist in Rehab, understood perfectly how awful my circumstances were. "You are living under intolerable conditions," she told me, but she couldn't do anything to help.

Both Andrea and Lisa were going to university away from Ottawa. As fall wore on, it came time for them to go. Before she left, Andrea told me to consider having two replacement visitors, Giselle and Susan. I considered the idea and decided to see my friends.

I had grown up with these girls and was really quite comfortable with them. Giselle is adorable. She is sweet, understanding, kind and giving. She is also one of the few people who was actually smaller than I am. She came to visit me one Sunday afternoon. I absolutely bawled when I saw her. She had obviously been prepared, probably by Andrea, for my reaction. My father explained, unnecessarily, "Judy understands everything. Her hearing and cognition are perfect." After that Giselle visited me weekly.

Sue looks sort of like me. She has long black hair and very pale skin. But she is tall and lanky, unlike me. We have been friends since high school. Sue didn't visit as often as Giselle did, but I was still totally comfortable with her.

It was while I was in Rehab that I finally started to visit at home. It wasn't especially magical. I hated the ride. I had to take a van service called ParaTranspo, which was very frightening. The vans lurched forward every time they stopped. I felt like my head would fall off. Of course I was always sad to return to Rehab. I would taste freedom for a few hours and then I'd go back to the prison where I lived.

I had personalized my hospital room as much as possible. I wanted it to reflect the real me. I wanted people to see me as real and vivid. I put photographs all over. I put Cassatt and Degas posters on my ceiling and walls. One of my aunts had made me a mobile of dancers and I hung it wherever I lived. I always had my purple floral duvet and lots of stuffed animals. My room was bright and cheery compared to the drab bareness of the hospital, but it was still a prison.

❖

I think perhaps the saddest time to be in the hospital is over Christmas. I don't even celebrate Christmas, yet I found it extremely sad. I spent two Christmases in Rehab. I felt so sorry for the poor patients who couldn't go home for Christmas. Often they couldn't even go home Christmas day. Tons of volunteers came in to give pathetic greetings. A hired Santa wished all the pitiful patients a hearty "Merry Christmas." He sauntered into my room to give me a ho-ho-ho and wish me a Merry Christmas. He was flustered when I couldn't even acknowledge him.

"Well, that's what you get for visiting a hospital on Christmas Day," I thought bitterly.

I was not at all appreciative.

I knew my stroke was worse than everyone else's in Rehab. I could see that. I knew how sick I was. I knew none of my friends had ever really suffered like this. It was so easy to feel sorry for myself. People couldn't believe my condition. I couldn't move, I couldn't talk. I was twenty years old, but I was exactly like a baby, except I could spell.

❖

Judy's mother: In Rehab, Judy was assigned to a room for four, close to the front desk. We all felt Judy would benefit from lots of company and activity, and the nurses could keep a better eye on her from nearby.

We had a battalion of people to get to know and work with. We were coordinating and facilitating all the time. Most days I'd be at Rehab twice, appearing first at lunch time and then again about 7:30 to visit with Judy until it was time for Judy to go to bed.

We were really Judy's ombudsmen and we had to keep on top of everything. It was demanding and exhausting, but the results were worthwhile. *The atmosphere in Rehab was very different from that in the hospital; there was a positive feeling of being rehabilitated instead of being treated like a patient. I was always talking to everyone about everything. I tried to ask the questions that I thought Judy would want to ask, plus satisfy my own curiosity. When you have a child who is completely helpless, you deliberately try to get everyone on board so that they will do their very best for her.*

We knew that if there was no therapy and no one visiting, there was nothing Judy could do. We tried to build in as much activity and stimulation as possible. Beginning the last month in the Ottawa General Hospital, we hired a reader to come in six days a week to read to Judy from 4:30 to 7:30.

Keeping in touch with her friends at Cornell was essential to Judy's mental and emotional well-being. She didn't want to lose the link to these wonderful friends from a life and time she had so adored. Never much of a letter-writer before — Judy believed in verbal communication — she now began to write everyone. She would dictate letters to her friends with the help of any willing partner. Visitors were often asked to "take dictation" as Judy spelled out her letters to her friends. These letters were often the first step at reestablishing a connection with her friends out of the city. Some would then come and visit.

Luc: *I started thinking about Judy's discharge planning right after she came to Rehab. Judy told me that her goals were to live in her own apartment and to walk again. I knew that the goal of walking again would be a very long time in coming, and my feeling was that we should work on the goals we could achieve. I also knew from personal experience how much independence means to someone in a wheelchair. When I broke my neck in 1979, there were no places for independent living in the community — only "homes" where people in my position would be cared for. For a number of years, I ended up living with my parents, and I had to fight hard to get into an apartment of my own. Judy was in the same boat — except that her condition demanded lots more care, which would have been too difficult for her parents to provide. I knew we were in for a big battle, because I knew all too well how little was out there in terms of facilities.*

Giselle: *It wasn't until several months after Judy had had her stroke that she was ready to see me. I felt prepared and strong from talking with Andrea, who had been visiting Judy regularly, as well as by keeping in touch with Judy's family. At this point, Judy was in Rehab. When I first saw Judy, her father met me at the door of* her room and brought me to see her. My first thought was "She looks just like Judy ... Judy looks so beautiful, she really does look beautiful." Her father kept encouraging me to touch her. This was hard for me to do because I wasn't sure how Judy felt, but I held her hand. Many early visits we spent crying and becoming reacquainted. Understanding and working through Judy's method of communication seemed complicated at first. However, it became easier to grasp as our visits became more and more frequent. I was amazed at the extent of our conversations, and many times I left Rehab feeling completely emotionally drained. I would spend the rest of the day thinking, "If I feel this way, how does Judy feel?"

Judy's mother: In November, after close to five months in the hospital and Rehab, we finally arranged for Judy to come home for an afternoon. That first trip home was both wonderful and sad. Ken and I drove to Rehab, and then I took ParaTranspo with Judy while Ken trailed us in the car. It was difficult for Judy to take this new mode of transportation for the first time; it reinforced how much her life had changed. Dear Luc, who has a wheel-chair accessible van for his own use, had offered to drive Judy both ways if that would make it easier on her. But we felt we had to take the plunge sometime, and it might as well be now.

Inside the van, we went through the necessary tying down of the wheelchair to the floor so it wouldn't move during the trip. We were the only passengers. When we got home, we struggled to get the chair and Judy up the two steps at our entrance and into the hallway. It was an emotional moment. Then we went into the kitchen. Judy immediately wanted to tell us something. She began spelling out "R-E-C-O-V-E-R ... " We jumped into the conversation, finishing her word and sentence. We talked animatedly about her recovery process, what it would entail, what we were hoping for from Rehab, etc., etc. Judy impatiently began spelling again — "R-E-C-O-V-E-R T-H-E K-I-T-C-H-E-N C-H-A-I-R-S!!!" We just howled with laughter. Here we thought she was talking about one thing when what she really was doing was reminding us that it was time to get rid of the chair coverings that she'd always hated! The rest of the visit was uneventful, and the first of many, many afternoon visits on the weekends.

Judy's father: Soon after Judy's first visit home, we started going out with Judy on trips sponsored by Rehab's recreation department. We came to have lots of experience with ParaTranspo; it runs very well and we used it frequently for the next two years.

Our first out-of-Rehab outings were to shopping centers in December. The first excursion was positively traumatic for mother and daughter. Anne was terrified that people would stare at Judy and she didn't know how she or Judy would handle that. As it turned out, some people did look, but more people didn't seem to see them at all.

Judy's mother: *I was aware of looking defiantly at anyone who dared to look too long in our direction in case it upset Judy. Judy was sensitive as well and at the end of our first expedition, she asked, "Aren't you embarrassed to be seen with me?" I was so elated at how well everything had gone that I was very eager to try another adventure soon. We also went to our first play at the National Arts Centre that December.*

Dr. Grinnell: *Judy was not the youngest person with stroke we'd ever seen in Rehab, but her stroke was the most severe. When she first came to Rehab, we had two very basic goals: to develop a seating system that would give her head control when she sat in a wheelchair and to develop some sort of switching device that would allow her to open a computer interface and thus communicate with more independence. We were not expecting to see any rapid change in her paralysis; our experience with other brain-stem stroke sufferers had taught us that any change would happen as the result of therapy over years, not in the months that Judy could expect to spend in Rehab. As time went on, another goal was discharging Judy not to a chronic-care hospital, but to a more independent setting that would allow her rehabilitation to continue. However, knowing that reaching this goal would be extremely difficult — facilities for independent placement of people in Judy's position did not exist in the community — we did not want to present it as a formal goal at first lest the disappointment be too great.*

EIGHT

"I quickly noticed one problem with eating.
I had to be fed."

I started to eat again in Rehab. I hadn't eaten in five months and I was more than ready! I didn't begin eating regular food, of course. I couldn't chew at all and had to prove to everyone that I could swallow. On the floor in the General Hospital I started eating ice chips and pudding. I was very excited. I told my parents I was craving alphaghetti. My mom was appalled. She had never bought a can of the stuff and couldn't imagine where I had ever tasted it. I knew Heinz would be pleased at my loyalty.

The first food I officially tried to eat was indeed alphaghetti. My parents brought it to me one night. But I was disappointed. All the pasta remained at the front of my mouth because my tongue and lips weren't working.

I quickly noticed one problem with eating. I had to be fed. It is most humiliating to be fed when you are in your twenties. It is not simple to feed me. I use special plastic spoons that won't break if I bite down on them. I need large mouthfuls placed at the back of my mouth to excite my swallowing reflex.

A friend of my mother named Jane had started visiting me in the General Hospital. She fed me lunch on Tuesdays and Thursdays. She was whimsical and eccentric. My mother fed me lunch on the other days when Jane didn't. This meant that I never had to be fed lunch by nurses, which was good because I hated being fed by most nurses.

It is infinitely better being fed by someone who cares about me. Nurses just mechanically shovel food into an opening. Most nurses never even asked my mother how to feed me. There is a certain knack to it, but most nurses assumed they already knew how to do it.

I spent a typical day at Rehab like this: I woke up around five a.m. after a terrible night's sleep. My primary nurse arrived at seven-thirty; at eight she got me dressed and ready for the day. Then I had breakfast. This consisted of instant cream of wheat and peanut butter. Once, Dr. Nelson visited me when I was eating this lovely concoction. He was quite fascinated. He went home and tried it. He liked it.

After breakfast, I had occupational therapy. It was extremely boring. I never did much of anything because Rehab was having a hard time finding any devices to help me return to normal function, like a call bell. After Rachelle left to have her baby in January, I got a new occupational therapist. Her name was Ann and I loved talking to her. She was bright and funny.

After occupational therapy, I had physiotherapy. In physio I did range of motion in my chair, sitting upright, and on a bed, lying supine. I had a new therapist named Patsy. Unlike me, she was calm and serene. I couldn't imagine how we'd ever get along. In point of fact, we got along fabulously. Physio was my favorite part of the day. I didn't actually like physio, but I adored Patsy. I think Patsy thought I was a little bit crazy. I was very light-hearted and cheerful despite the ghastliness of my condition. I was also very dramatic. Every day, I would give Patsy the low-down on the nursing situation. If I had had a new nurse, I would describe how that nurse had almost killed me. I was not patient with new nurses.

After physio, I had lunch. The food at the Rehab Centre was the usual institutional fare — not very imaginative or tasty — so my parents supplied some from home. If Jane was there to feed me, I ate food from the fridge that my parents had brought in. I drank jellied juice. This was juice with gelatin added to make it a very thick consistency. My mother always had some juice prepared in the fridge.

After lunch I had speech therapy, and after speech therapy, I would lie down for several hours. My parents arranged for me to have a reader or a tutor every day from about four until seven. At night I had visitors. Sometimes it was my parents and sometimes it was a friend. It might be Giselle or Sue or Rosemary or Isabel.

Visitors were very important. I lived for the moment when the next visitor arrived. Next best were phone calls from friends.

I was supposed to go to bed at nine p.m., but the nurses never got around to me until around ten o'clock. One of my nightly rituals was to pick clothes for the next morning. Whoever happened to be visiting me at night performed this duty. One night when my father was visiting, I told him I wanted to wear my azalea sweater. I had ordered that sweater from a catalogue and it had been called "colour: azalea." My poor father nearly went nuts trying to find my azalea sweater. Neither one of us will ever forget that incident.

❖

Judy's mother: Although Judy had started swallowing while she was in the hospital, we had been cautioned that she might always require her tube for feeding and fluids. Once she got to Rehab, the work began in earnest to get Judy eating as much as possible. Both eating and swallowing are in the province of speech therapy, and we worked with two wonderful therapists. For several months, Judy had daily sessions to work on her eating.

First, we had to help Judy open her mouth wide enough to get a special spoon in her mouth. Judy would sometimes bite down as an uncontrollable reflex, so the spoon had to be flexible enough to protect her teeth. Once her mouth had food in it, she then had to swallow what was there. We learned that big mouthfuls stimulated the swallowing reflex, and we would put in generous tablespoons full of soft, easy-to-swallow foods. Then we'd have to make sure that nothing was left in her mouth, or on the roof of her mouth, because she couldn't move her tongue to manipulate the food.

Everyone was enthusiastic about Judy eating again and got involved in furthering her progress. I began to bring in things like Creme Caramel, and in the afternoons, the nurses would indulge Judy with treats from the cafeteria; Judy and her friends still talk about the wonderful day Judy discovered date bars. The Rehab kitchen posted menus in advance and we could choose each week's meals for Judy, informing them of any special requirements. They always tried to puree anything she wanted. I used my food processor a lot. It was a delight to give Judy back her joy of eating.

Some of our earliest outings from Rehab were to restaurants. We'd phone ahead to be sure they were accessible to wheelchairs and that the kitchen would be capable of chopping up Judy's food. We discovered that it was best to bring along our own food processor and have the restaurant use it to chop Judy's food.

Our first restaurant outing — to a nearby Red Lobster — was with a group from Rehab on one of the regular Thursday night outings organized by the Recreation Department. It was a huge success. The restaurant staff were extraordinary in their efforts to prepare Judy's food and to please us. They were relaxed and acted as if it was totally unremarkable to be asked to chop up a patron's food and then wash the food processor to boot! We sat at a table with one of Judy's younger roommates and had a very nice dinner. We were all relieved that it had gone so well, and this set in motion a lot of restaurant outings of our own as well others with the recreation group from Rehab.

We found we were able to go almost everywhere and the people were anxious to be helpful and accommodating. The one exception was a Chinese restaurant that was not eager to use a food processor. Undaunted, I brought along a small hand-operated nut chopper that worked by pressing a blade up and down. As a group of us sat around the table in that restaurant, I was bent over the food chopper on the floor, chopping away. I don't know what the other diners thought of this performance, but I thought it was pretty funny. Judy got her Chinese food and we all had a good time.

Lunch time was a very slow time at Rehab because half of the staff would be eating and the rest would be feeding patients and meeting other pressing needs. As Judy began to eat more and more, it was necessary for staff to feed her, too. Ken came when he could get away from work, but I would come and spend most lunch hours with Judy. That gave me the chance to touch base with the doctors and therapists who were seeing her that day. However, this cut a large chunk out of my work days on Mondays, Wednesdays, and Fridays. On Tuesdays and Thursdays my dear friend Jane came and visited with Judy. Jane's kindness and generosity cannot be overestimated. She could be relied upon to keep Judy amused, write letters with her, talk to staff and roommates, and keep us informed. It meant that two days a week I could have lunch with friends at work.

There were two areas of great confusion and concern with Judy's care: communication and feeding. Both were much more easily demonstrated than described, so, during the winter of '92, in cooperation with the speech pathologist, Sue Carroll-Thomas, we made a video of Judy with me demonstrating both the feeding and communication. It was a great success!

There were both a TV and a VCR in the nurses' room at Rehab and they could use the video to ease a new nurse into the intricacies of Judy's care. It also served to help regular staff, who may not have had the experience of feeding Judy, know what to expect. One question was how much to feed Judy at any one time. The normal instinct was to put just a little food on the spoon in case Judy choked or coughed. That was just the opposite of what worked best. Judy needs large mouthfuls to stimulate her swallowing. Also, Judy has never choked on anything. She has a great gag reflex and coughs beautifully. That can intimidate a nurse, but seeing it happen with her mother on the video was very reassuring.

The telephone had always been an essential part of Judy's pre-stroke existence and this was not to change. We got a phone put in Judy's room and set up a system so she could call her friends and receive calls from them. A "phone partner" would dial or receive the call and then place the phone to Judy's ear. When it was in place, we'd say, "Okay," and the caller would begin talking. When Judy had a comment to add or a question to ask, she'd bat her eyes and we'd tell the caller, "Just a minute, Judy wants to say something." Then Judy would spell out her message and the conversation would resume. This method preserved the confidentiality of her caller's conversation without annoying her roommates, but as soon as Judy moved into her apartment, we got speaker phones, which were a great improvement.

One new feature of life now that Judy was in Rehab was that she could once again wear clothes. In the hospital we had quickly moved from hospital gowns to Judy's own nighties. Once she was in Rehab, she continued to wear her nighties at night, but now she could wear regular clothes during the day. Nothing could have made Judy happier. We were asked to bring clothes that had elastic waists and tops that were easy to take on and off. Fortunately the closet in her room was large, because over the one and a half years she lived in Rehab, she acquired quite the wardrobe! We felt that it was a way of feeling like herself—Judy had always loved clothes and shopping and had very firm ideas about what she liked to wear—and it gave her a sense of control to be able to keep up with fashion and choose her outfit for the next day.

NINE

*"I decided that it was much better to be
educated and locked in."*

In January, six months after I had my stroke, I had recovered
enough to decide what to do about school. I would complete my
undergraduate degree in psychology, which I had begun at Cornell.
I had already been having readers for a while, but they had been
reading me fiction instead of course material. I obviously didn't
know my prognosis but I decided that it was much better to be
educated and locked in than to be uneducated and locked in.

Cornell was extremely helpful. It seems that the school was
just as amazed at my circumstances as I was. Also, my advisor,
Professor James Maas, happened to be the director of the Psychology
Department. That first winter in Rehab, I took a correspondence
course in the psychology of sex roles. The lectures were taped for
me by my friends, and my tutors or readers read the course work
to me. The content of the course books sometimes led to funny
situations. For instance, one of my roommates was very shocked
and told my parents that my tutor was reading me pornography! I
was very grateful to Cornell for allowing me to continue my courses.
My friends brought me lecture notes and tapes when they visited.

Until this time, I hadn't wanted to see any of my college friends.
I thought that the effects of the stroke would be temporary and
didn't want to scare them. But now, seven months after my stroke,
I decided it was time to see my Cornell friends. Kelly, Carrie, and
Julie were my three dearest friends from Cornell. We had all lived
on the same floor freshman year and had had a terrific time. They
had been calling regularly since my stroke but couldn't possibly be
prepared for the new me.

They were supposed to come up on a Saturday, but we had a huge snowstorm that weekend. They surprised me by appearing on Sunday after making the five-hour drive from Ithaca. I cried even before they arrived. I cried the entire time they visited. I was wearing a pink sweater and purple sweat pants.

"I remember that sweater," Carrie exclaimed.

Kelly did nothing but cry.

"Julie, " I spelled, "I saw you. . . . "

She sobbed.

". . . last summer. I didn't know if you saw me."

We tried to pretend I hadn't had a stroke. We tried to have a conversation just like old times, but it was hard to talk when I had to spell everything. Kelly kept hugging and kissing me and crying. She still smelled the same. I was overcome with emotion. In all our time at school, I had never seen my friends cry like this. I had known this moment would be difficult. Later, our visits would get easier. I wrote afterwards:

Dear Kelly,

When you were here yesterday, I told you two lies. I was too scared to tell you the truth because I thought you might kill me! Firstly, I think chocolate does stain. I'm really sorry because I know I got it all over you. Secondly, I do not have a cold; I always cough when I eat. Many nurses have found out the hard way: never stand in front of me when I'm eating. . . .

Love,
Judy

The most significant factor in my recovery was the role of my friends. In Ottawa, there were Giselle, Sue, Karen, Erica, Isabel and Kim. In Ithaca, there were Kelly, Carrie, Julie K, Julie G, Beth, Gabrielle, Kim, and Lori. Away at school were Lisa, Susanna, Kim, Andrea, and Lauren. I lived for visits from my friends. My Cornell friends visited on weekends. I can't stress enough how important friends are to a patient's recovery. I honestly don't know how I would have survived the many months in a hospital without my friends. They made the dullness bearable.

I can't imagine being an elderly person with a stroke like mine. It's the loneliest feeling imaginable. There were some elderly people who went week after week without visitors. I couldn't think of a more desperate situation. I guess those people just learned to ignore it.

Actually, I can't imagine any person having a stroke like mine. Nobody, not even my parents, understood how I felt. And I'm one of the luckiest ones. I saw stroke patients every day who were frail and depressed. I must have seemed the same way. I cried all the time. We all hated being like this.

❖

Judy's parents: After her stroke, Judy missed her friends and the academic program at Cornell terribly. In keeping with her wish to finish her degree, we contacted the Psychology Department at Cornell about setting up a correspondence course for Judy. As the news of Judy's stroke spread at Cornell, the university was very supportive — and gratified to learn that Judy was interested in continuing her education.

Cornell did not have a system of correspondence courses in place, so we had to work out a plan with Professor Maas. Because Judy was unable to read, her sorority sisters volunteered to read all of the text work into a tape recorder so Judy would be able to hear the course material. Professor Sandra Bem, who was teaching a course on the psychology of sex roles, was eager to help and agreed to have her lectures tape recorded as she was giving them. The tapes were then sent to Judy in Rehab.

This provided Judy with a focus while she was in Rehab. Her daily reader, Gil, also read her some of her textbooks. By the summer, having spent the winter and spring of 1991 working with a tutor, Judy was ready for the exam. Professor Bem sent us the exam, which was all short answer, and Judy's tutor administered it over several days. There was wonderful support and encouragement from everyone at Cornell and Judy was thrilled to resume working on her degree.

Dr. Maas: Judy had often stopped by my office to chat after her summer statistics class, expressing an interest in getting to know my family and offering to baby-sit if my wife and I ever needed help. Before she could visit our home, however, I received a call from Tompkins Community Hospital, where Judy had been taken by her roommate. When I went to the hospital, I met Judy's parents and learned that Judy — this beautiful, vibrant young woman — was very sick. It was not until some time later that we were informed that Judy had suffered a severe stroke.

I will never forget the day when Judy's mother called me to discuss Judy's desire to continue her education. Incredible! What a fantastic idea! But was it realistic? Like most major universities, Cornell has specific and rather rigid residency requirements — students have to attend classes on campus to receive credits. However, the University responded with great and appropriate sensitivity to Judy's extraordinary motivation and unique circumstances. All of the faculty we approached were willing to have their lectures recorded on audio-tape and to make multiple choice exams available to Judy for off-campus credit.

Gabrielle M: *I first met Judy at Cornell University's sorority rush; we lived in the same sorority house. We spent a lot of time together — talking, laughing, back-scratching, gossiping. And we went to class and studied. Judy spoke French, was obsessed with having sweet-smelling hands, had a boyfriend and tons of girlfriends, danced, did well in school and had a blast on spring break. Life was good. No, life was great. And then our sophomore year ended and life changed.*

After a whirlwind of confusion and disbelief — and the shock of learning that Judy had had a stroke and would not be back in the fall, or even the following spring — we were able to visit her in the hospital. Our friend Beth and I decided to make the trip to Ottawa. Having heard reports about the teary-eyed visits of Kelly, Carrie, and Julie, I was really nervous about seeing Judy.

Judy's mom briefed us on Judy's condition and her communication system. Then we went up to the hospital to see Judy. Up, up, up we walked, up two flights of stairs, all the time wishing they would go on just a little longer. Entering the second floor of the hospital, we met Judy. The new Judy. At first glance, she was hardly recognizable physically. Her makeup had been applied by a nurse who clearly was not skilled in that area. Her long braid was tied to a neck support at the back of the wheel chair to hold her head up. But her eyes were the same. Though not as clear and steady as they had been in the past, they were still the same warm eyes of the Judy who went to formals and danced and gossiped and laughed and chattered away until her eyes would no longer stay open.

Lori I: *When I heard from a mutual friend that something was wrong with Judy, that she had had some kind of aneurysm or something, I called the hospital in Ithaca, expecting to hear that everything was fine. No one would give me a straight answer. It was extremely scary and frustrating, but still, I could not imagine that Judy was in severe danger. I remember telling some friends that at least this had happened at the beginning of the summer, so Judy would have time to recuperate before fall classes began.*

The severity of the situation began to sink in as the summer went on, and we learned that Judy had suffered a brain-stem stroke and that her road to recovery would be a long one. We all began to realize that Judy would not be coming back to Cornell in the fall. Judy was not ready to see us, so we wrote to her and received information about her condition.

The next semester, I went to see Judy in the Rehabilitation Centre a few times. Those visits were quite upsetting, because though friends who had visited her earlier prepared me to see her, I somehow expected Judy to be the same smiling friend I had had — and when I got there she didn't smile or speak or move at all.

Nevertheless, I learned her communication code, and we would sit and talk by her bed or in the hall or over in the main hospital's cafeteria. Even though this was a hospital and Judy was sick, we did find things to laugh at. For example, when Julie and I took Judy for a walk outside and got totally lost; we should have known better than to follow Judy's directions, since it had been weeks before she could find her way to class from our sorority house at Cornell. Anyway, we ended up having to lift Judy and her wheelchair over a curb. Judy found this pretty hysterical, considering that Julie and I are not exactly big brawny types.

Luc: *Judy had a hard time in Rehab for a number of reasons: she had had the worst stroke the staff had seen, and they had to learn to spell with her in order to communicate. Quite a number of them did not, even though there was usually a spelling chart taped to Judy's wheelchair and at her bedside. Finding the right equipment, such as a reliable call bell or a workable head support for her wheelchair, was difficult at best and impossible at worst, leading to more frustration. At the same time, because Judy was totally paralyzed, the staff did not get the feedback they were used to — there was no body language or change in facial expression to help them judge how their efforts were being received.*

TEN

" I'd rather die than go to St. Vincent's."

IN January 1991, my parents visited a girl named Susan in Baltimore, Maryland. She'd had a stroke exactly like mine ten years before at the young age of twenty-three. She too had been on birth control pills. She was now, after ten years, starting to walk. Ten years was an awfully long time but at least this was something concrete. Susan was my inspiration. She wrote me often and told me of her progress. Now, years after her stroke, she was able to work, to go camping, horseback riding, even skydiving. Nothing had moved on her either for the first couple of years after her stroke. In her letters she told me how slow her recovery had been and that recovery can only be achieved through very hard work.

I wrote her to say she was the only person who truly believed I would get better. Nobody here knew anything. Susan had started to write and had sent me a valentine. It was very inspiring.

Susan said that physiotherapy was the most important thing in her life. I was not exactly thrilled to learn this.

I felt burdened by the severity of my condition. The worst part was definitely being unable to talk. Nurses could and did ignore me. I fluttered my eyes when I wanted to spell, but unless someone was watching my eyes and was prepared and willing to spell with me, I was ignored. Especially when I wanted to get ready for bed did I find that nurses ignored me. They would leave me alone in my room for several hours. I couldn't remind them that I existed so I had to wait — to be moved, to be dressed in my nightgown, to have the light turned off — the frustration welling in me. They were always apologizing after they noticed me.

"How long have you been waiting?" they would ask, not really caring. I would raise my eyes and think, "If only you knew. . . . "

❖

It was about this time that I first heard of St. Vincent's. This was a chronic-care hospital in Ottawa for very elderly people who could not care for themselves. I desperately did not want to go there. Canada has a government health insurance plan and the normal medical course for an individual after a stroke like mine was to go to St. Vincent's. There was only a single, remote possibility of avoiding this fate. This was to write to the provincial government and convince them that I didn't belong in an institution. My parents and Luc had the fight of their lives.

It really was an amazing feat to persuade the authorities that I should be allowed to live in my own apartment instead of a chronic-care hospital. No one in my position had successfully managed to find an independent placement.

Living independently was a non-traditional and unconventional and completely novel idea, especially since there was no other facility available. For that reason, I was required to have a preadmission interview for St. Vincent's, even though I was adamant about not living there upon my discharge from Rehab.

While I was waiting for the province to decide my fate, I decided to write a book about my experience with the stroke, the hospital, and Rehab. Partially, the writing served as a catharsis. My emotions were positively raging after having been hospitalized for so long, and writing became an outlet for my frustrations. Also, hardly anyone knew anything about locked-in syndrome. I felt it was up to me to teach people. The one deterrent was my method of communication. Since I cannot move or speak and can only communicate by spelling with eye blinks, the process was slow, laborious, exhausting, frustrating, tedious. But writing this book was something I felt I must do.

I really wanted to reach young people who are involved with birth control pills. I don't think people realize how dangerous birth control pills can be. All the young women I know either take the pill or have done so in the past. I just assumed that I too would take the pill. No doctor ever warned me that I could have a devastating stroke.

John and I were so incredibly stupid not to be alarmed by my severe headaches. I really thought I was invincible. I never in my wildest dreams imagined that anything like this could happen to me. I think most healthy people must feel this way.

❖

Judy's parents: During the months immediately after Judy's stroke, we were desperate for information about other locked-in cases. We needed some basis for understanding Judy's condition and some guidance for her future recovery. We were not very successful in finding other cases that were comparable, especially people Judy's age. Most of the cases we heard about were older patients who did not live long after their strokes.

At the same time, people were also sending us information about communications systems. We were in touch with specialists who adapted computers for use by people who couldn't speak. We received an article that described a Morse code system that had been devised for patients with brain-stem strokes. It contained a description of a clinical case of a young woman who had had a brain stem stroke in 1981, when she was twenty-four. She was living at home, in the Baltimore area. This was the closest we had come to finding a match for Judy.

The author was Woodrow Seamone, of the Applied Physics Laboratory at Johns Hopkins University. We contacted him to find out more about the clinical case he had identified in the article as "S."

That is how we found Susan. We called her parents and told them about Judy. In January 1991, we arranged to go to Baltimore to visit Susan and her family. At that point, it had been ten years since Susan's stroke.

We were warmly embraced by the family. Susan was living at home with her parents and was proficient on a computer that she activated with switches attached to her thumbs. By moving her thumbs, she used the long and short dashes of Morse code to spell words that were displayed on her computer screen.

Susan was an inspiration to us. There were many parallels to Judy: she was female, young, had been on birth control pills, and was at university when her stroke happened, although she hadn't had migraines. She was the only suitable person we had found for trying to arrive at a prognosis for Judy. When we met her, Susan could move her thumbs. She had "gross motor movement" and could move her arms and legs. She worked hard at physiotherapy and had recently begun to take steps; with the aid of a walker, she was able to walk across her family room.

We wanted to know how and when Susan's changes came about. Were they gradual or sudden? What had the doctors said? What had her prognosis been? Did both thumbs start to move at the same time? The family's message to us was simple and direct: The doctors don't know, the body and brain are always changing, and body functions do and will come back. We returned to Judy with more optimism than either of us had felt since this ordeal had begun.

The average patient's stay in Rehab was between six and nine months, although some did stay longer. We had initially been told that Judy would probably stay a year because of the severity of her stroke. However, Rehab was definitely not a facility for long-term patients; it existed to prepare people to return home as soon as possible after a stroke or accident. Thus, the Rehab Centre was required to have some plan in motion for all their patients, as, sooner or later, all would need to be discharged. In Judy's case, her limited physical abilities and her heavy care needs made it necessary to think of a chronic-care hospital. We were told that her name would have to go on the waiting list for a local chronic-care hospital, St. Vincent's.

In Ottawa at that time, there was no resource other than St. Vincent's available to a young person in Judy's condition. Putting Judy's name on the St. Vincent's list was not our plan, but we had to go along with it — or at least appear to go along with it — while we were trying to set up something we felt would be more suitable. Judy's physical needs might have indicated chronic care, but we knew that her mental and emotional needs called for a situation that afforded her more independence and control. We also felt that Judy would just give up if St. Vincent's was to be her fate.

We decided to go and see St. Vincent's so we could be as informed and knowledgeable as possible. We had actually heard many good things about this hospital from friends whose elderly parents were receiving care there. The staff and facility were praised and the programming was said to be comprehensive. However, it was an old building, full of elderly people, with no special facility or ward for the younger patients in the building. It wasn't the right setting for a vibrant 21-year-old, and we knew that we'd have to try and arrange something else. We didn't tell Judy of our visit at that time; she would have been mortified to think that we were plotting to put her away in a chronic-care institution. If there had ever been any doubts, that visit to St. Vincent's ended forever any thoughts we might have entertained for Judy moving there and only confirmed us in our intention to move her into her own living arrangement.

After our visit to St. Vincent's — and especially after the required interview with an admissions nurse — we felt we should fight for full-time nursing and attendant care in an apartment. Although the nurse was very understanding and sympathetic to our situation, the interview was very upsetting. We were galvanized into action and began in earnest to prepare the request for an Order-in-Council — an official variation from established regulations that can be granted by a government Minister. We decided to proceed with Judy's discharge planning as if we had, or were sure we would receive, the assistance we sought from the government.

Throughout the ordeal of Judy's stroke, the Ontario Health Insurance Plan never let us down. At no time during Judy's hospitalization were we ever confronted with a financial obstacle to her treatment. The procedures that Judy underwent were discussed with us by her doctors and decisions to proceed or not were dictated by medical considerations and what would be in Judy's best interest.

We had heard of families in the United States being forced into bankruptcy when faced with catastrophic medical events like strokes or cancer. We were fortunate to be living under a system of universal health insurance which did not add the burden of financial worries to our other concerns.

The effort to get Judy out of a hospital setting and into the community was mostly a struggle to align the various programs of community and social support into a package tailored to Judy's special requirements. To its credit, the health-care system was, if anything, over-protective in its reluctance to release Judy into the community until there were assurances that she would be properly cared for.

We justified our request by demonstrating that Judy did not fulfill the definition of a chronic-care patient. Judy was showing herself to be a young woman with a lot of interests and abilities; she was taking university courses by correspondence, and she was leaving the Rehab Centre to go to concerts, plays, and restaurants. Her friends and family were involving her in loads of activities and Judy was eager to do as much as possible. Once Judy began to request weekends away from Rehab on a regular basis, we set up outside nursing for her and demonstrated that with the right kind of help, Judy could manage very nicely in the community.

We had a great deal of support for these weekends from both the Rehab Centre and the Outreach Program of the provincial government,

*who provided some funding for weekend nursing. We were build-
ing our case and hoping we would be successful. We requested that
Judy be a pilot project for the Ontario government, which was itself
at a crossroads in developing a long-term care policy for more community care. We asked our friends, the mayor of our city, members of
the federal and provincial parliament, university officers, and other
people who were in positions of influence to write on Judy's behalf.*

Dear Minister:

We have been impressed with and grateful for the Ontario
health services made available to our daughter over the past
year. We are fortunate to live in a province where the quality of
care and support services is so high and accessible. However,
we are at a point in Judy's recovery where the services available
will not meet her future needs after being discharged.

The professionals at the Ottawa Rehabilitation Centre who
have worked with Judy since her admission and are fully
knowledgeable of all available resources and support services
in Ottawa-Carleton suggested that Judy's needs, future growth
and recovery would be best served by applying for an Order-
in-Council. This most unusual request by the Rehabilitation
Centre is a reflection of the unusual and unique nature of Judy's
situation and their belief in her ability to flourish in the community with full-time attendant care. It is also a reflection of
how inappropriate it would be to confine a young woman of
Judy's age and ability to a chronic-care institution.

... We are requesting that this application be granted at a time
when the province is beginning to formulate a policy on long-
term care. We have been told that in the future a person in
Judy's situation would not fit the criteria for chronic institutionalized care. Judy offers a good opportunity to help in the
formulation of this policy as a "pilot project." We will provide as much information and data as requested to help in this
planning process.

In exchange, Judy will have quality of life that will enable her
to complete her education and make her contribution to soci-
ety. Her determination and positive outlook have not wavered
during this past difficult year.

> Sincerely,
> Ken and Anne Mozersky

Luc: *I knew from the first that St. Vincent's wasn't the right place for a very smart young woman like Judy, and the entire team at Rehab — Dr. Grinnell, the therapists, the psychologist, etc. — all agreed that she wouldn't continue to make progress in a chronic-care hospital, where the emphasis would be on maintenance rather than stimulation.*

I knew we'd have to apply for an Order-in-Council and immediately began putting together the information we'd need — reports from the doctors at Rehab, plus estimates of nursing care and therapy requirements and costs. Judy and her parents asked friends to write letters testifying to Judy's need for an independent placement. Meanwhile, Judy was required to undergo an interview for possible admission to St. Vincent's, and even though the nurse who conducted the interview was very nice and clearly sympathetic, the interview itself served as a chilling reminder that institutionalized chronic care was the grim and likely reality for Judy. I think recognition of that harsh reality made us work even harder. At the same time, I knew the chances of our getting an Order-in-Council were slim at best, because the costs involved in Judy's care were so high. But at the very least, by applying for an Order-in Council, we'd get a foot in the door — the Ministry of Health would become aware of Judy's existence and know that some kind of provision would have to be made for her.

ELEVEN

*"Canada has a wonderful health care sys-
tem — until you want to get out."*

By the early spring, my social worker Luc had put together a
report which was a request for an Order-in-Council and sent it to
the Ontario Government. In it he had explained why I didn't belong
in a chronic-care hospital. It was quite a long report. It read in part:

> ... The Order-in-Council for Judy means far more than the
> physical acquisition of attendant care needs. ... It means for
> Judy a future where none existed before. Further, it would per-
> mit her to savour a world of numerous possibilities: selecting
> university courses, planning and hoping for work one day, and
> dreaming about her future. It would allow Judy to be an active
> and useful member of society. ...

> If Judy is to live on her own ... [she] will be able to develop
> a sense of self-reliance and self-esteem that she will never ex-
> perience if she is placed in a chronic-care facility. ... If an
> Order-in-Council permits her to be accepted into the academic
> world, the working community, and society at large, Judy will
> emerge from a position of total dependence and resignation to
> one of self-motivated independence. It will certainly encour-
> age Judy into a world that precludes any notion of defeatism
> and will have opened the door to her future ...

> ... Medical science has provided Judy the opportunity to live;
> however, no avenues have previously been opened to her
> wherein she could begin to have some semblance of a life free of
> institutions. Judy is very excited about the possibility of living
> in her own apartment. The acquisition of an Order-in-Council
> would give Judy this opportunity.

The provincial government was asked to help me with twenty-
four hour attendant care in an apartment instead of chronic-care in

a hospital. The government immediately refused. I thought my world was collapsing. I was being betrayed. But I did not know by whom.

My parents decided to appeal the decision.

I absolutely admired my parents for their strength in this matter. They were vehemently refused at every level of government. They were adamant, however, that I did not belong in a chronic-care institution. And they never gave up.

As I look back on that time, I realize that my parents were truly exceptional. At a time when I was little more than a body to be fed and cleaned, they appreciated my mind. They understood that I couldn't live in an institution, at the mercy of routines and schedules designed for people decades older than me. My parents assured me that I was going to an apartment. My sweet father claimed that he would never let me be institutionalized. My strong mother was fighting for my freedom.

The whole process lasted a year and a half, during which time I was in my "favorite" place, Rehab. By the fourteenth month of this uncertain future, I was taking tranquilizers regularly. I was a miserable mess.

❖

As the months dragged on, many of my Rehab nurses did not believe that I would avoid St. Vincent's. They used to secretly prepare me for the indignities of a life in chronic care. "Of course you must have a male nurse," they would taunt. "At St. Vincent's, you will have many male nurses."

I especially didn't like male nurses because so much of what I required a nurse to do was my personal grooming. A male nurse simply couldn't do any of this. I was also totally uncomfortable being dressed and undressed by male nurses who were practically my own age. Unlike most people who have had strokes, I could feel and was aware of everything. The hospital couldn't understand this. I had to fight wickedly to be assigned only female nurses and I wasn't always successful.

I was having a horrible time with the head nurse in Rehab. She made me switch rooms because she didn't want to rearrange the nursing schedule so I could avoid male nurses. She was very inflexible. Following my good experience with Hazel in Neuro-Obs, this was a nightmare.

At one point, I became so frustrated and angry and disappointed that I went on strike. I refused to do any therapy activities for two weeks. My protest was an example of my need to have some control over some part of my life. Nobody questioned my little rebellion because it was typical of my character. Unfortunately, I had no power and no rights. My only element of control was whether I would go to therapy cheerfully. Thus I went on strike.

I had a nice time at first. I did nothing but lie in bed all day. However, I got bored. Because of this I wanted continuous visitors. I was a terrible patient. I was unhappy and manipulative in my idleness. Eventually, I got tired of just lying in bed and ended my strike.

The months dragged on. Time crawled. Each day was bleaker and more dreary than the last because my situation did not change. A year after my stroke, I still had no call bell and thus no way to call a nurse if I was thirsty or needed to have my clothes changed or was in pain from sitting in the same position for hours. I thought I'd never get out of Rehab. My stay seemed interminable.

❖

While we were waiting for a reply from the province, my parents pretended I'd already gotten the Order-in-Council and began to plan for an apartment.

If I was to have my own place, I would need my own nurses. I had to interview several before I found one I liked. My mother contacted a number of nursing agencies and explained my require-ments. As a result, I'd found my first nurse: a girl named BJ. She was young and blond and pretty and kind. BJ was not at all like my Rehab nurses. Some of them were fake and short-fused.

As soon as I found her I started to go out on the weekends. I usually went to a place called the ILU, which stands for Independent Living Unit. This was a nice apartment in the actual hospital that was designed to help people who had suffered some accident or disability prepare to live in the community. It was lovely. Now when my Cornell friends visited they slept over at the ILU. We slept two in my bed. Once when Beth and Lori were visiting, we slept three in my bed because we are all small. We wanted so much for things to be the way they had been at Cornell, where we all used to lie in bed together when we were napping or on lazy mornings. At Cornell, my bed was often piled so high with junk that I couldn't crawl into it and instead would find myself a willing partner and squeeze into bed with her.

Sometimes I would have friends visit me in the ILU and sometimes I would just spend the evening with BJ. My friends all really liked BJ. It was important that my friends get along with my nurse since I would be spending so much time with her.

The ILU visits were heavenly. So were the occasional weekends I spent in local hotels when the ILU was not available. Since BJ was my only nurse at the time, she always accompanied me to hotels. Sometimes my mom stayed over, too. The hotel staff were always courteous and extremely gracious. I think they all felt sorry for me.

I definitely wanted to be without a feeding tube by the time I left Rehab, so I had to work on increasing my fluid intake. When my friends came to visit, they got used to finding jellied juices in the Rehab fridge and helping me drink.

Dear Carrie,

Hi! I'm writing this as a tubeless person! They removed my stomach tube this morning. I'm very excited because they said they'd never be able to remove it. I hope you and Julie can visit next weekend. . . .

Love,
Judy

❖

Luc: When the original request was turned down, we immediately appealed. We also went to see the Minister for Health, whose office then made some phone calls on behalf of our cause to the Community and Social Service Agencies. Earlier, officials at those agencies had told us that they were sorry, but there was nothing they could do: Judy was stuck with her situation. The Minister suggested that all involved change their focus — instead of looking to one ministry to provide for all of Judy's needs, we should look for a solution that used resources available from a variety of government agencies.

Dr. Grinnell: Although it's true that Judy did feel very vulnerable, at the mercy of the nursing staff, it's also true that the Centre's staff is relatively small and that male nurses are an inescapable part of the equation. If the one R.N. scheduled for a particular evening happened to be male, it would have been very difficult to juggle the schedule just for Judy. And to put the shoe on the other foot, for years, men with disabilities similar in degree to Judy's have had no choice but to accept care from female nurses and attendants.

With all the difficulties and delays in putting together Judy's discharge plans and in finding appropriate appliances such as a workable call bell and a wheelchair with adequate head support — which were diffficult to find, despite advances in technology — we weren't surprised that Judy decided to "go on strike." After all the time she had spent in Rehab, seeing little in the way of functional recovery, she needed to take a break from her therapies and other rehabilitative activities — to spend more time at her parents' house, in the hospital's independent living unit, or in hotels outside of Rehab. Afterwards, we made a joint decision that while Judy would of course continue physiotherapy to maintain her condition and keep her muscles from getting tight, she could postpone more ambitious physio until she was settled in a new situation and felt more motivated.

Judy's parents: The first bit of success came when the head of community resources for the disabled assured us that if the funding for nursing came through, Judy could have an apartment in one of several buildings in Ottawa with attendant care available to back up her nursing care. We, Luc, and Dr. Grinnell spoke with people in several different governmental departments about Judy's special needs. We had to keep things moving so everything would be in place the moment our request was granted. We knew we couldn't just sit back and accept what seemed to be the inevitable. "Assert yourself. Show some gumption," Judy would blink out to encourage us in our struggles.

As time went by, and Judy's eating had moved from purees to mashes to small pieces, we were able to take her out to restaurants and just cut her food up at the table, rather than using a food processor.

Fluids presented a different kind of problem. Everyone was careful to give Judy a lot of fluids so that she stayed healthy and avoided developing either bladder or skin problems. This was easy with her stomach tube: you just filled a plastic fluid bag with juice or water, and with the twist of a valve, it would empty into Judy by gravity.

But Judy wanted to be without a feeding tube, which meant that she had to be able to drink adequate amounts of fluid — and fluids are hard to manage when you don't have control of your mouth or tongue. *We tried a variety of things to get fluids into Judy by mouth. Jellied juices were prepared to a gelatin-like consistency and fed to her easily, by spoon. The next step was to try juices that were thickened with a special thickener. We also tried giving her juices orally, using a squeezable plastic bottle with a small spout; we would squirt the liquid into her mouth. The fastest method was to use jellied juices.*

As we got closer to getting her out of Rehab, Judy was adamant that she wanted to be "tubeless," although the adults in her life were a little more cautious. Our biggest concern was that she might not drink enough and would become ill. Judy, however, showed the same determination about this as she had earlier, when she wanted to get rid of her trache. Finally it was decided that Judy could have her tube removed — if she could manage the requisite amount of fluids, now to be taken as jellied juices. In January of 1992, she had reached the point where her doctor, after much consultation, finally felt that Judy would be able to manage without her tube.

Judy was already taking pills, such as aspirin to prevent another stoke, by mouth, so her medications were not a concern. And for Judy to have this control over her own drinking and diet — and thus her life — would be a triumph. Once she was able to maintain her fluid intake at an acceptable level for an acceptable period of time, we got the go-ahead to remove the tube.

We took Judy over to the Ottawa General Hospital, where we were met by the surgeon who had implanted the tube a year and a half before. Then the back of Judy's throat was frozen with a spray to lessen the gagging and irritation from the light and camera going down her esophagus to her stomach on a tube. Once they were inside, we could see inside Judy's stomach and the inner portion of her feeding tube. Grasping the inside portion, the surgeon cut the tube in half and both portions were removed — one from the inside and one from the outside. Voila! Judy was tubeless and triumphant! ! As Dr. Grinnell so accurately put it later that day, "Judy just loves thumbing her nose at the medical establishment!" After that, the opening in Judy's stomach closed quickly on its own.

Even after Judy had her feeding tube removed, however, getting enough fluids remained a concern. Over the months, Judy had grown tired of all the usual juices — cranberry, orange, apple, grape. The Rehab kitchen had a limited variety of juices they could gel for her, so the ball was in our court to find new flavours. Jellied water tasted awful so we went to jellied teas. We tried many varieties of tea as well as the more exotic juices, such as kiwi-strawberry. We would prepare these jellied juices, using gelatin, and bring them to the Rehab kitchen. Spooning unjellied liquids into Judy's mouth was very time-consuming — but worth it, for the joy of a hot (actually, warm) cup of tea.

TWELVE

"My fate is completely in the hands of the government. How terrific!"

AT first, the government turned down my parents' appeal for re-consideration of the Order-in-Council. The provincial government refused to grant me full-time nursing care. I then asked all my friends to write letters stating why I didn't belong in a chronic-care hospital. I even received letters of support from people I thought didn't even know I'd had a stroke.

Eventually, the provincial government sort of succumbed to the pressure. They would provide some of the care I would need. My parents would have to provide the rest.

The day the provincial government agreed with the plan for me to live in an apartment with a roommate, my friend Karen happened to be visiting me. She immediately said she would be happy to be my roommate. Karen and I had gone to France together after grade twelve and had enjoyed ourselves on the sunbathed beaches of the French Riviera. Now we would be roommates.

By March, 1992, I had been hospitalized for twenty months. I was supposed to leave Rehab at the end of April. Once I knew I would be going to my own apartment, I couldn't wait to be free. Rehab and its rules were driving me crazy.

Dear Beth,

... I need some sympathy. I absolutely hate it here.

I have been in the hospital almost as long as I was at Cornell. That is ridiculous.

... I can't stand this atmosphere any more! Everyone here is old and dying. I try to stay positive but it's hard when you live in this environment.

I'm not getting along with my nurses. It's so bad that I've hired my own private nurse. I won't describe my nurse problems because they are too petty . . .

Love, Judy

Dear Peter,

Hi! How are you? I'm not great. I'm still stuck in this hospital indefinitely. If you want to know the details ask my mom.

I was just home for the weekend. It was nice but it's always a let-down to come back here . . .

Love,
Judy

I couldn't wait to move into my apartment. I couldn't wait to leave the cold impersonal, sick, tainted hospital atmosphere. I had little in common with most of the nurses in Rehab. I think they were appalled that this could happen to such a young girl. Although they sympathized with me, they were, for the most part, much older. The worst part was having to spend twenty-four hours a day with them. And my occupational therapists had not yet found me a workable call bell. It had been nearly two years after my stroke and I still had no way to call for help. It was extremely frightening and frustrating not to be able to call a nurse when I needed one.

One of the Rehab nurses told me how much I'd miss the hospital when I moved to my apartment. I doubted that. I could not imagine missing Rehab. An apartment would be far superior. In an apartment I could have so much more control over my life.

One event that I had dreaded was graduation. In spring of 1992 my college friends graduated from Cornell. I didn't want to go down to Ithaca for it.

Dear Lori,

. . . I'm getting so depressed about graduation. I wish Cornell would just let me graduate. I seriously can't deal with the thought of you guys graduating.

. . . My nursing is going terribly. Rehab is trying to introduce me to male nurses. I just don't feel comfortable having a strange guy undress me, even if he does have an R.N. beside his name. So I am making a huge fuss.

Love,
Judy

Dear Beth,

It is graduation in about a month and it's making me totally depressed. I start to cry every time I think about it. I just can't deal with this at all. I wish Cornell would just let me graduate. . . .

Love,
Judy

Dear Carrie,

. . . I just thought I'd tell you what is going on here. I still haven't moved, nor do I have a discharge date. I'm moving to the independent living unit next weekend for a week, on a trial basis.

Things are very, very hard for me right now . . . First, I'm living in a hellish environment. I can't seem to get out of here. Every day is worse than the day before. You can't possibly imagine how depressing an atmosphere this is. I try to focus on the positive things but I can't always. I know things will get much better, but right now, it's so hard.

Second, I can't deal with this upcoming graduation. I am taking it so badly. . . . I've wasted two years of my life here, had the worst luck, and it all culminates in a lousy graduation. Sometimes I get so upset I just cry hysterically for hours and wonder why I didn't just die when I had this stroke. We know it was severe enough. . . .

Love,
Judy

Dear Kim,

Please thank whoever thought to include me on the senior tea invitation. That was so kind. It made my whole day, it really did.

Things here are pretty dismal. It looks like I will spend graduation in the hospital. In case graduation itself isn't depressing enough, Rehab sure is.

Don't expect me to be all upbeat because I'm not a happy camper.

Love,
Judy

The actual graduation day was horrible. It was raining and gloomy. I talked to Beth, Kim and Lori that night. They, of course, told me how awful graduation had been—but what else would they tell a friend who was supposed to graduate with them but couldn't?

While we waited for my discharge date, my parents were looking into getting me a wheelchair-accessible van. Getting a van would mean I could travel to visit all my friends. A bunch of them lived in New York City. Kelly lived in Boston. Carrie and Julie lived near Ithaca. I also intended to visit my relatives in Washington. ParaTranspo was a great service but it required twenty-four hours advance booking. One couldn't be spontaneous twenty-four hours ahead. It was just impossible. My own van would allow me spontaneity.

It was now early June. I was scheduled to move into my own apartment in a month, but I had been supposed to move since November and I was skeptical. We had gotten the province to agree to provide some nursing, but it took a while before an appropriate apartment became available. One apartment that I really liked had been available earlier, but my wheelchair wouldn't fit through the bedroom door!

Dear Carrie,

I have some good news at last! I have an apartment for sure, for sure, on July first. This horrible episode in my life is finally coming to an end. Thank God! I am finding some wonderful nurses and I have an apartment and a discharge date. I think everything is finally coming together. . . .

Love,
Judy

By this point, I was utterly frustrated and disgusted with life in the Rehab Centre. I simply couldn't handle the struggles over nursing and the lack of control anymore. To get around this situation, I started having a personal nurse come in every morning. In addition to BJ, there were now Karen and Stephanie. Karen was the sister of my friend Giselle's boyfriend. Stephanie had been a student nurse at the Rehab Centre and I met her there. I loved my nurses and I looked forward to working with them when I moved.

The most important function of a nurse and the reason I had a personal nurse was to spell. I couldn't make a noise and the regular Rehab nurses were so overworked and busy they rarely spelled with me. Nights in Rehab were just terrible. Two nurses were assigned to take care of an entire floor of thirty people. My sleeping was horrible and I often awoke in the wee hours and needed a nurse. They were supposed to check me every hour, but I was lucky if they came three times a night. I had had my own night sitter in the General Hospital. When I got to Rehab, however, they took away my sitter. Rehab thought I'd be more "independent" without a sitter. This left me with exactly no way to call for help for eight hours out of twenty-four

About this time, my parents and I heard from Dr. Vaillancourt. He inquired hesitantly about my health. My parents wrote and told him. He sent me a letter and said he wished to keep in touch with me. He would be teaching at Stonybrook on Long Island. I intended to have the friends who lived in New York visit Dr. Vaillancourt.

Also about this time, I learned that Patsy, my physio, was pregnant. I thought of her as much too young to have a baby. I thought of Patsy as being my age. I was certainly not prepared to have a baby, but then again, I wasn't married.

I thought about marriage a lot when I was in Rehab. Luc had become paraplegic at about the same age as I had my stroke. When I asked what he thought about marriage, he said that although it would certainly be more difficult now, I shouldn't automatically close that door. One day my father was looking at me and turned to my mother.

"I think she will have to marry a neurologist," he pronounced. "Or a male nurse."

❖

By this point I had basically lost touch with my ex-boyfriend John. I knew that he was still at Cornell and I knew that he wasn't doing well. I also knew that I did not want to see him. From the moment I became locked in, I didn't want a boyfriend. The idea is very frightening when one can't move or utter a sound.

One weekend when I was in the ILU, my dad read me an article. It said that fearlessness was a privilege of the young. How I knew this to be true. This stroke had made me feel old. I was no longer fearless. In fact, I was very fearful. I was scared of everything.

I remember when my speech therapist, Sue, took me to the Ottawa General Hospital to see the newborn babies. They were very tiny and cute. A nurse held up a sick male baby. "I know how you feel, baby," I thought with smugness. "You can't talk, either. All your muscle movement is involuntary. I'm exactly like you, baby." This I found quite interesting: the person I identified best with was an infant.

I suppose other people see me as a baby, too. My mother read me an article about another woman who had a brain-stem stroke. After ten years, she had recovered nothing. This was a very dismal prospect. I was living with an impossible condition. I guessed I would have to confront my situation more fully when I moved out of Rehab.

❖

Luc: Even when the appeal was turned down, we wouldn't take no for an answer. We spent the summer and fall negotiating in marathon meetings involving people from the DPCR, the Community Services Outreach agency, the Social Services Administration. There was something of a crisis in October, when Judy's name finally came to the top of the waiting list for St. Vincent's. But because we were still working on various aspects of Judy's rehabilitation — getting her a switching device and a workable wheelchair — as well as her discharge plan, we made a team decision not to send Judy to St. Vincent's. Finally, our negotiations started bearing fruit, as all the agencies gave a little. The Health Ministry made an exception to their usual policies and offered nine hours of nursing care; we got some time from the Home Care administration for homemaking and cooking; the family's insurance could offer a bit, Vocational Rehabilitation Services offered a few hours, and the DPCR offered attendant care.

Judy's parents: Nothing fell into place at once. The province would say one thing, and we'd make a counter offer. We had a number of long, protracted meetings at Rehab, often with as many as twenty people all involved in the case and eager for a successful resolution. Luc was our captain, and his supervisor, Zora, was behind him. It helped that the local Member of the Provincial Parliament was also in the Cabinet. She sent her representatives to some of our meetings. The breakthrough came, after many months, when we worked out a plan that provided nursing care for half the day, with a roommate in the apartment and an attendant on call at night; the family would support the rest. We could now proceed with our plan to have Judy live "independently" in the community.

Dr. Grinnell: The situation for Judy in Rehab was very difficult. Judy certainly felt thwarted, but so did the health-care professionals — doctors, therapists, nurses — trying to help her. Nothing is more frustrating for people in health care than not being able to make a situation better, whether because of difficulties with the system, the existing technology, or the people involved. In addition, because the Rehabilitation Centre is part of a teaching hospital, many of the people with whom Judy came in contact were just starting out in their careers. Some of them found Judy's physical limitations hard to accept; when you're twenty-one yourself and you're dealing with another twenty-one-year-old who's been paralyzed by a stroke, it's hard not to feel, "There but for the grace of God go I" and get very upset when you can't make things better in any material way. On the other hand, some staff dealt with the same feelings by distancing themselves — and Judy, who is very people-oriented, would have felt that acutely.

Luc: Judy had been on the DPCR waiting list for eight months, and it took some time for her name to come to the top. Of course, Judy was impatient with the pace of all of this. She been in Rehab for a long time without seeing much change in her condition, she had seen a number of her roommates discharged, and her friends graduating from college and moving on in their lives. She wanted to be moving on, too.

THIRTEEN

" I was so glad to be free."

I finally moved into my apartment in early July of 1992. Two years had elapsed since my stroke. Someone I knew had just been admitted to Intensive Care at the Ottawa General Hospital after a car accident. His hell was just beginning. I would not trade places with him for anything. Even with my future so uncertain, I was happier being me and leaving hospital life.

I was so excited! The plan was that BJ would be with me all that evening and the next morning too. It seemed sort of fitting that she be with me when I left the Rehab Centre because she had known me longer than any of the other nurses who would be working with me.

The next morning, many Rehab nurses bid me farewell, including one nurse who pretended not to know that I despised her. This poor nurse had once committed the crime of running a brush through my freshly permed hair. There was a certain amount of confusion as I left. As one nurse kissed me good-bye, another misplaced my medicine.

We all waited outside for the ParaTranspo van to take me to my apartment—my mother, my father, BJ, and me.

"Well, we did it," said my mother victoriously. "We got her out."

My father smiled. A feeling of peaceful elation was upon us.

I watched the ParaTranspo van pull up to the curb. I still bore scars from my stomach tube and my tracheostomy. My mother kissed me and got out her camera. Some things never change. I guess she wanted to remember this momentous occasion. BJ traveled on the van with me. I was really leaving the hospital and Rehab.

My new apartment was ideally located — across from a mall and near tons of restaurants. My apartment was just as I expected. A bouquet of flowers greeted me as I entered my bedroom. I had picked out my bedspread and curtains sophomore year at Cornell. The living room still looked very barren. My parents had chosen very plain, very beige furniture. Karen and I hadn't decorated yet and we really needed to. The summer we spent in France seemed like ages ago. I couldn't believe how much had happened in the five years since then. I had gone to Cornell, I had had a stroke, I had been in Intensive Care, I had been on a respirator. I had been in the hospital for so long.

The next day, my nurse Stephanie came and relieved BJ. In the evening, my mother, my father, my brother, my aunt, my uncle, my cousins, and my grandmother all came over. They all wanted to see where I'd be living.

Finally, my roommate Karen arrived. She brought her boyfriend and a friend of his. There were so many people in my apartment. Having an apartment represented the epitome of freedom.

I thought of St. Vincent's with a shudder. Did anyone actually like it there? I couldn't believe that people without articulate, well-educated relatives fighting for them had no choice but to be institutionalized. I felt so sorry for those poor people. In an institution the rules are so stringent. One eats when and what the institution is serving. One visits when and where the institution allows guests. One rests when the institution dictates. This was no way to live.

I was so glad to be free.

Canada fortunately has universal health care. I can honestly say, however, that if this universal health-care system involves putting people in institutions I am vehemently opposed to it. I lived in an institution for over two years — and I wanted to die. I'm not even clinically depressed, nor was I ever. I'm not an unhappy person. In fact, I'm quite happy, despite the horror of my situation. It was simply that living in an institutional environment made me want to die. I only recount this sad fact to illustrate the ugliness of institutionalization and to show how even a non-depressed individual can want to die. It wasn't the Ottawa Rehabilitation Centre, per se, that was so awful. It is all rehab centers. It is, in fact, all institutions.

I had absolutely loved Cornell. I had loved my freedom and my independence. Now I was completely dependent for everything. My parents wanted me to be as independent as possible. That is why it was so important that I get my own apartment. I could not imagine life in a chronic-care hospital.

> Dear Michelle,
>
> It was great to hear from you. I have now moved out of the Rehab Centre and into my own apartment. It's been a long haul and now I'm perfectly content. . . . I'm living with my friend Karen. We are having a blast! . . . I have nurses taking care of me all day but I don't mind a bit because they are so nice.
>
> > Take care,
> > Judy

After nineteen months in Rehab, I could hardly believe that I was finally living in an apartment. The services in the apartment building where I live include attendants. These are young men and women who work out of an apartment in the building and take care of people in wheelchairs. I have nurses, so I just need the attendants to help transfer me in and out of bed. Some of the attendants are close to my age and I enjoy that.

This is how I spend a typical day: I usually wake up very early. My day nurse appears at seven a.m. Sometimes I want to rest more, and sometimes I want to talk. At eight o'clock I usually eat breakfast. My nurse feeds me in bed. After breakfast, I have a bed bath, a lengthy ordeal that takes about two hours. I don't like showers because I get too cold. If I want to go out, we use the van. If I want to stay in, I can write letters or have a book or newspaper read to me or call a friend on the phone. Sometimes I have a tutoring session instead, or physiotherapy. My physiotherapist comes three times a week, but I do a bit on my own every day. I can sit in my wheelchair for about three hours at a time; after that, I need to lie down to rest and change position.

My evening nurse arrives at three o'clock in the afternoon. If I want to go out, I eat supper between five and seven p.m. I sometimes go to restaurants and ballets, plays, or movies. Often a friend visits in the evening. Then my nurse gets me ready for bed. My night attendant comes in at eleven. I still don't sleep very well, and sometimes I talk until morning. Sometimes a friend stays over.

I have three full-time nurses and several part-time nurses. Each of my nurses has had her own special talent. Stephanie was my cooking nurse. She and I would try anything. We would find recipes in cookbooks and were eager to try them. Stephanie's family had told her that she was a terrible cook but I thought she was just fine. BJ is my spelling nurse. She is the best at communicating with me. I always enjoy going out with BJ because she is so adept at knowing what I want. Perhaps this is because she has known me so long.

Karen G was my everything nurse. She was literally good at everything — talking, spelling, shopping, cooking, writing, and reading. I loved doing anything with Karen G.

I don't mind having a nurse with me at all times. My nurses are all quite young. They don't wear uniforms and when we go out, it looks like I'm out with a friend. And I am, since I never think of them as nurses at all. I think of them as friends who take care of me. One nurse said to me, "Judy, you are my only friend whom I put to bed."

In addition to nurses, I have tutors. My first tutor was a terrific young woman named Danielle. She came four times a week. She was extremely understanding and baked me many desserts. She would partake in everything I did during her stay. If I went to the store, she came along with my nurse. If I went to a restaurant for a snack, Danielle ate too. Danielle was an excellent tutor for me because she herself was a psychology major at nearby Carleton University.

My next tutor was my nurse Karen G's sister, Sue. She, too, became a friend as well as a tutor. She was always willing to join in my various activities.

I am continuing to take courses toward my degree in psychology and I enjoy having newspapers and books read to me. I have always liked human interest stories, and now, perhaps because of my own situation, I especially enjoy biographies and autobiographies of people coping with difficult circumstances.

I am thrilled to be in my own apartment, and much happier than I ever was in Rehab. And I continue to make progress. For instance, my drinking has improved significantly. A few months after I moved into my apartment, I was at the mall having a muffin with Stephanie.

"Here, I want to try something," Steph said.

She put away my jellied juice and held a cup to my lips. I actually drank a liquid from a cup. "Yay!" I thought. I hadn't had a liquid in over two years. I had had first a tube in my nose, then a tube in my stomach, then I drank jellied juice. Now I was finally swallowing fluids.

In the months I have been out of Rehab, I have really made my apartment into a home, with lots of bright colours and artwork everywhere. The mobile of ballet figures that my aunt brought me when I was in the hospital came home with me. I was very much complimented recently when Dr. Nelson said that although others had done the decorating, my apartment is all me.

I have also become a mall rat since leaving Rehab. My apartment building is located next to a mall. I quickly fell into the habit of going to the mall for a convenient change of scenery. The mall is great for this because it is so close and it is accessible to wheelchairs.

Soon after I moved into my apartment, my wheelchair-accessible van was ready. It has a lowered floor and ramp which allows my wheelchair to fit inside. It allows me spontaneity that I never had with ParaTranspo. The company that modified my Dodge mini-van was named "Freedom Motors." My van has brought me exactly that — freedom. I can now go out to eat, to visit, to see a play on my own schedule.

❖

Judy's parents: When Judy moved into her apartment we felt both relief and trepidation. We were glad that she was out of the hospital and we felt a sense of accomplishment for having gotten her into an apartment. But this was all new territory for us. We didn't know if the living arrangements would prove satisfactory, whether the attendants in the building would be able to communicate with Judy, nor how her roommate would work out. Judy had selected her first team of nurses and we had asked them to do their own scheduling. We didn't know if this would be feasible, although it has all worked out better than we could have hoped. We thought we would often have to fill in at night or during day shifts at the apartment because of scheduling mishaps. In fact, this has happened only rarely.

Karen G: I am Judy's nurse but we have something of a personal history as well, having gone to the same elementary and high schools. My brother's girlfriend is also one of Judy's close friends.

When I heard that Judy had had a stroke, I remember feeling heartbroken and confused about her exact condition; I did not learn more about Judy until almost two years later when Judy was looking for a nurse and wondered if I would be interested.

I met with Judy for the first time on a Sunday afternoon while Judy and her nurse BJ were visiting her parents' home. BJ and I had been at university together, which made my first visit a little bit easier. I remember preparing myself to meet Judy, fearing I would be shocked to see her in a wheelchair, unable to move or converse. I was surprised to see the same young woman I had connected with in passing so many years before. She didn't look frail or sickly as I had feared, but beautiful. As soon as we met I felt our hearts touch and I knew it would be difficult to separate the personal from the professional.

It took a little while for me to get used to Judy's method of communicating through eye blinks. I made mistakes but it still went fairly quickly because half of the time Judy and I were thinking the same thing and I could guess her thoughts.

I learned Judy's personal care as well. It was not difficult to learn, but Judy was extremely picky about the way things were done. It didn't take me long to realize that my nursing priorities had to change for Judy. Judy was not very interested in such subjects as skin breakdown, range of motion exercises, proper positioning, medication, nutrition, or thorough nursing assessment. Judy was more interested in hairstyles, make-up, clothing, friends, and the telephone. We tried to balance all of these. Judy occasionally gave me time to perform traditional nursing duties, and I, in turn, learned to use a lip brush to apply lipstick.

I began to realize that for me, this was real nursing. The traditional tasks associated with nursing are not always the most important considerations for everyone. The needs of the 'patient' have to be met, and Judy has the needs that all other young women in their twenties have. Sometimes she just fails to realize that she has other special needs associated with being the victim of a severe brain-stem stroke. We usually worked these things out — and Judy usually got her way!

Danielle: When I started tutoring Judy, she was living in the Rehab Centre, in a room with three other patients. One of the other women in the room eavesdropped constantly and would comment on the book I was reading if she saw fit. This gave me an idea of the amount of privacy Judy had.

It seemed to take me an eternity to learn her communication system. For the first month or so Judy and I hardly spelled at all. In time she began to tell me about herself before her stroke and to share her thoughts about life in Rehab. I also got to know her through reading her mail to her and taking down replies, and by meeting her friends. I saw her parents when they came to visit her, and they treated her just like a healthy person, which helped me to do the same.

In a short time, I began to feel quite necessary to Judy: if she was lonely, I provided company; if she was bored, I amused her; if she was uncomfortable, I rang for a nurse. In time, I even learned how to feed her. Judy's mom had written a detailed explanation of how to feed her, and Judy vastly preferred being fed by a friend to being fed by a nurse, so I just took over at dinner one night. I guess I had a knack for it because I ended up feeding her during most of my visits. Her favorite food was the illicit date squares she'd have me get from the cafeteria — illicit because the cafeteria staff didn't know Judy could swallow and suspected me of eating them, and because Judy could slam back three or four in a row if they let me take that many.

In my mind, I changed from tutor to companion, reading her magazines as well as course work, taking dictation for letters and her book, fixing her hair and make-up, and feeding her and changing her position in bed when she was uncomfortable. These new activities, especially the ones that involved touching her, helped me to see her as a person rather than as a patient, and impressed upon me that she was a basically healthy, typical young woman like myself, despite the fact that she couldn't move. I saw us as very similar indeed, and marveled that one of us got up and walked out of the room each evening, and the other stayed. The roles could just as easily have been reversed.

Tutoring Judy in Rehab was almost an oxymoron. We got a pathetically small amount of work done that first year. In addition to the fact that Judy needed me to do many things beside school work, there were constant interruptions by nurses, therapists, and other hospital staff — constant invasions of her privacy with which Judy coped by perceiving the absurdity of the situation and laughing at it. By the time Judy left Rehab to move into her own apartment, I felt that both my job description and our relationship changed. Since Judy had private nurses, I no longer needed to do so much for Judy's care or comfort, and there were fewer interruptions. It took Judy a while to get in gear for serious school work, but when she did, we got a lot done. We soon completed the course we'd begun in Rehab and moved on to new ones.

Sue G: The course I was hired to tutor was Abnormal Psychology. My job was to convey the lecture material to Judy and to administer the exam. When Judy and I first started working together, we used to study for a few minutes and then Judy would ask me if I wanted to go for a walk or to the mall. I didn't mind doing these things with Judy and in fact they helped me to get to know her a little better. I was, however, concerned that we wouldn't get through all the material she needed in order to write her exam. Eventually, we were able to study for three or more hours, with only a few short breaks.

Working with Judy was a challenge. In an effort to add more stimulation and variety to my teaching, I found myself making a lot of eye contact with Judy in order to make sure that she was keeping up with my reading and that she understood the material, and I began modifying the tone and loudness of my voice. I found that the greater enthusiasm I had for the material, the more alert Judy seemed to be. I also supplemented the course material; while we were studying eating disorders, for example, I stopped and asked Judy if she had any friends who may have had eating disorders and what role she thought the media played in the etiology of the disorder.

Judy is a very intelligent and perceptive young woman. When I gave her the exams in their multiple-choice format, I often found myself challenging her choice in answers. As a psychology major, I was quite familiar with the material and wanted to make sure that she understood the reasoning behind her answers. Judy never failed to defend her choice or position with material that I myself could recall only vaguely from the readings.

Judy is also one of the funniest people I have ever met. I found that the more she was able to communicate her feelings, the better she felt, and we'd often end a tutoring session laughing hysterically.

Dr. Maas: To date, Judy has taken several psychology courses, including a sex roles course in women's studies, a cognitive psychology course, and a course on the psychology of sports. Judy prefers writing essays to taking multiple choice and short-answer tests, even though that requires a tremendous amount of time and effort. She is determined to finish her major and will be aided tremendously when she finds *the type of computer that will enable her to communicate more efficiently.*

FOURTEEN

"Right now the idea of walking is completely foreign to me."

SOON after I moved to my apartment, Dr. Grinnell and I decided that it was time for more physiotherapy. I didn't really focus on physiotherapy while I was in Rehab because I was obsessed with my discharge. In fact, I had been so frustrated the last several months that I had done only the basics to keep my muscles from getting tight. Now that I was in my own apartment, I was much more motivated to do serious physio.

My new therapist is a gifted woman named Diana. She is dynamic and perky in spirit. She truly believes I will move my body again someday. She told me she intends to do weight-bearing exercises with me. She is very creative and has novel ideas.

Susan, the girl in Maryland who had the same kind of stroke as mine, also had a super physiotherapist and Diana has talked to her.

It took Susan nine years to take a first step. Nine years is such a long time not to walk. I hope I take less time.

Right now the idea of walking is completely foreign to me. I can't even hold my head up by myself. Diana is working on that. She tries the most interesting things. She bounces me on a small trampoline and puts me on my stomach to facilitate certain reflexes. She also lays me over a giant orange ball. She then has me try to move. There were eleven people watching me the first time I tried this. Talk about pressure! Diana says I lifted my head and arms but I didn't feel anything.

Since my stroke, I have grown four inches taller! I am no longer short. I used to be 5'2" and now I am 5'6". People have various theories as to why this has happened. Some claim that the spine relaxes and expands when it rests for so long. Others claim that my pituitary gland was affected by the pill and the stroke. Whatever the reason, I am overjoyed to be taller. Susan, the young woman in Baltimore who also had a brain-stem stroke, got taller too.

It is very hard to keep working on physiotherapy when it's so hard to see any change. Sometimes Diana will tell me that a muscle I've been trying to flex has actually moved, but I can't feel it. People also tell me that I've gradually regained some facial expression in the time since my stroke. My nurse Karen says she can always judge my mood by looking at my face. Personally, I think I look as placid as ever.

Not long ago, my girlfriend Sue came over to visit. She said that some people are getting frustrated because I'm not getting better. This made me furious. I am getting better! It just requires tons of patience. What do people expect? I had a massive, completely devastating stroke. Most people who can't move part of their bodies develop bedsores or pressure sores. These are irritating red welts that cover an immobile person as a result of the lack of sensation. Fortunately, I have full sensation and I've never had a bed sore.

I'm currently trying a treatment that involves putting electrodes on my trunk every night. They deliver mild current. This treatment is supposed to strengthen muscles. It works for cerebral palsy and spina bifida patients, but obviously no one with locked-in syndrome has ever tried it before. I haven't noticed a lot of changes, but Diana says I have more overall body tone, which is a very positive sign.

Not long ago, I learned that a doctor in California has discovered a protein that regenerates nerves. It is still experimental, though, and it will be several years before humans can try it. At this point, I cannot even entertain the possibility of my being cured. Nevertheless, I am excited at the prospect of trying this treatment.

Recently, I went to visit Dr. Grinnell. She was delighted by my progress since I've been in my apartment. I know that Diana has been talking to Dr. Grinnell a lot. I got the feeling that Dr. Grinnell thinks I will get better eventually. I never got that feeling from a doctor before. I have to get better. I just can't stay like this forever.

❖

Diana W: I was asked to see Judy at home by Dr. Grinnell, who felt the time was right for more physio. When I was given the information about Judy's stroke, I realized that this physiotherapy case was going to be different: I had never treated anyone with this type of stroke before, and I needed help. I did a computer search on locked-in syndrome and then found that one of the therapists on our service had treated a girl in England a few years before; and Judy told me about a physio who had come up from the States on a consult to see her when she was in Rehab. So, armed with information from a phone call to Arlene Greenspan-Crutcher, a physio in Atlanta, and my colleagues in Ottawa, we got started.

The initial goal was to provide maintenance care and to work with the nurses on a home program. But when I first saw Judy for an assessment, I felt we had to at least try to facilitate some active movement; her total inability to produce any voluntary movement with the exception of blinking her eyes and effecting a minimal muscle contraction in her left shoulder just felt overwhelmingly unacceptable. I felt that if Judy could twitch her left shoulder muscle, perhaps she could twitch somewhere else; anyway, with Dr. Grinnell's support, we decided we had to try. I told Judy and her parents that I did not know if we would get any significant improvement and that we should treat any recovery as a bonus. I was very concerned not to raise anyone's hopes inappropriately.

Treatment consists of trying to activate the muscles in Judy's trunk to give her some central stability — without which any movement recovered at the limbs and head would be useless, something like a rag doll which can only sit or stand up if you hold her in the middle. My colleague Janet and I work with Judy's nurses to help her to move, the intention being to stimulate her abdominal and back muscles. These muscle groups join the pelvic and shoulder girdles with the rib cage and spine to form the basis for human movement; they allow us to work against gravity.

Judy is sometimes afraid when we need to try new things, but she always makes the effort. We put Judy into a sitting position on the side of the bed and have her sit cross-legged on the bed, which she likes best. We also do more demanding activities, involving the ball and the trampoline, or standing up with splints on her legs to keep her knees from bending — all to stimulate some extension in Judy's back and neck and increase the abdominal muscle tone to give her the beginning of postural support. We also work on her limbs to try to facilitate some activity, especially at the hips and shoulders; we have to start in the center and work outwards.

We have made some progress, enough to justify increasing Judy's treatment from two hours to three hours a week — and enough so that with a little help, Judy can hold her head up and turn it from side to side when we work in sitting and standing positions. And, with a little help, Judy can also bend her elbows and straighten them. She can sit with minimal help; occasionally, we can take the support away altogether.

Judy also tried a system of low-intensity muscle stimulation which has been developed at the MaGee Clinic in Toronto. This involves placing electrodes over certain muscle groups; these muscles are simulated overnight while Judy sleeps. The hope is that this will lead to increased muscle tone.

We don't know where all this therapy will lead; the final outcome is a big question mark. But Judy is a fighter, and her positive approach to her life, along with her family's great support, gives us a head start. It will continue to be a team effort, with everyone working together everyday. We will work with Judy as long as we see improvements and she wants us there — we're in it for the long haul!

Karen G: In the time I have worked with Judy, her physical condition has improved slowly. When I first met Judy she didn't have any facial expression at all. Now Judy's expression can tell you subtly if she is happy, sad, frustrated, nervous, or furious. Judy's physiotherapist works very hard to help Judy regain and improve her muscle control. There have been resulting steps made toward increased muscle activity. These gains seem very small to Judy because right now they are weak and inconsistent, but they really are leaps and bounds in the right direction.

Dr. Grinnell: No one is prepared to tell Judy that her condition won't get better; that just can't be predicted. Most brain-stem stroke survivors show steady improvement over time, but there is simply no way to know how far it will go; there can be great recovery of functions, but nothing is guaranteed either way. In some individuals, some functions may come back over time, while in others they do not, in spite of hard and conscientious work. Beyond that, the way that rehabilitation proceeds is by way of constant monitoring and reassessment: it's only as we see what a patient can do that we can see what we might help them do next.

In Judy's case, there are reasonable grounds to be somewhat optimistic. In the time since her stroke, Judy has put her optimism about recovery in perspective. Yes, there will be more improvement, but over the long haul. Rather than expecting immediate and obvious recovery, Judy now seems to understand that things will improve — but over time. The big challenge for Judy and those working with her, such as Diana, is maintaining motivation. The physical changes

and improvements that Diana sees are quite real, and they offer reason for optimism, but from Judy's point of view, they do not count
as real because they haven't as yet led to changes in her functional
abilities. She can twitch a few more muscles, and her trunk strength
has increased, but this has not allowed her to use a call bell or take
a step, and this is very frustrating for her. The fact of the matter is
that the work facing Judy is bloody tedious, hard, and repetitive —
and Judy may feel that activities other than physiotherapy are more
gratifying.

FIFTEEN

"Do you know what I miss the most?
Touching other people."

I am "locked in," but most people don't know what that means. Locked-in syndrome is very rare, and there is very little literature available on it. Maybe this book will encourage further research.

I have been corresponding with Dr. Fred Plum, a neurologist from the Cornell Medical School. He had visited me when I was in ICU. He actually coined the phrase "locked-in syndrome." Unfortunately, this phrase describes me perfectly: I can't move or speak, but I'm fully conscious, cognitively perfect, and have full sensation.

I never know how to describe myself. I am not merely disabled or quadriplegic or aphasic. I am all of these things encompassed in one condition. I have quadriplegia, mutism, paralysis of facial muscles, and loss of horizontal eye movements.

My eyes are terrible. They don't move side to side at all. In addition, my eyes bounce up and down, though this has improved over time. My palate inside my mouth also bounces. This bouncing, which is called nystagmus, makes it impossible for me to read. I also see lights and shapes and spots in front of my right eye — green and purple masses and scintillating dots of white light. I have otherwise normal peripheral vision and this helps somewhat.

I have essentially no facial expression. At first people find this rather disturbing. Eventually they become accustomed to it. And I no longer cry when I see a mirror. The big advantage to my lack of facial expression, and the sole advantage to having locked-in syndrome, is that I will never get wrinkles on my face.

Being paralyzed is very strange. I wake up every single day and notice that I can't move or speak. I don't think I'll ever get so used to being in this condition that I come to expect it. I look down at my arms and I will them to budge, but they remain still. Sometimes people think that I can't move because I don't try hard enough, but they are wrong.

One Saturday afternoon not long ago, I went to see a ballet. That in itself is not significant for I go to ballets often. I was expecting to see the National Ballet perform "Giselle." It turned out to be a dance class rehearsal instead. I had not witnessed a dance class for several years. In fact, I was a member of the last dance class I witnessed.

Nobody would ever know this to look at me now, but I used to dance. I was never a serious dancer who devoted her whole life to ballet, but I loved dancing. At the dance rehearsal that afternoon, each time the ballet instructor on stage would describe the dancers' movements my feet got very excited because they remembered the familiar steps.

Now I am a motionless lump. I have been since June, 1990. I used to spent countless hours dancing. I did ballet, character, jazz, and modern dance. My mom was at the Arts Centre with me that day and I'm sure she felt just as melancholy as I did. A dancer who can't move. Life is ironic and strange.

I have always asked the question "Why me?" about the stroke, but I have always been more stunned than angry at the fact of it.

❖

I could spend forever and ever analyzing the psychological effects of this stroke. The question I get asked the most is:

"How come you don't get depressed?"

The simple answer is "I don't know."

When I was in ICU I was very shocked and scared and unhappy. Fortunately, my unhappiness was situational and these feelings went away once I left ICU. When I was in Rehab, I was so frustrated at the rules and the fact that so few people seemed to want to make the effort to communicate with me that I wanted to die.

I was, of course, urged to see a psychiatrist to help me cope with the psychological devastation of the stroke, but none of them could spell with me! My inability to speak was an obvious barrier to psychotherapy, so I became my own psychiatrist. I was friendly with the hospital chaplain, but it wasn't a counseling relationship.

Sometimes I get very down and sad and I feel sorry for myself. It just hits me that I can't do anything by myself and I become overwhelmed. Fortunately, this happens only rarely. My nurse BJ claims that it would be hard for her to work with me so closely if I were depressed. I too would have difficulty caring for someone who cried and complained all the time.

Although I had my previous world shattered in one day, although I lived in depths of misery and sadness, I am too happy a person to become depressed.

To pass in one day from moving to not moving, speaking to not speaking, eating to not eating, hearing to not hearing, breathing to not breathing, going to school to not going to school, having a boyfriend to not having a boyfriend, living in a sorority house to living in a hospital, is traumatic. I lost all that at once. So why didn't I die of depression? I really don't know.

I suppose it is due to the full support I received and continue to receive. My friends are terrific and call, write, and visit. And my family is amazing, especially my parents. I knew they were committed to me but I never knew how much. It took something like this to convince me of the depth of their feelings for me. This may sound selfish or sick or warped but I know that my parents will do anything for me. This must be why I never became depressed.

This stroke has changed the way I think and study. Before I was a visual learner. Now that I can't read or fall back on visualizing pages and memorizing, I am forced to pay very close attention to underlying concepts. When I take tests, it is much easier technically for me to answer multiple choice or true and false questions since I can just look up for "yes" and down for "no." However, I really, really enjoy writing essays. Since I have no facial expression, no use of gesture and no voice, I must express myself solely through words. I have grown to love language, writing and words. My communication system makes my life exciting and challenging.

I think of everything in terms of spelled words. Whenever I hear a new name, I inquire as to its spelling. When people can't spell with me, my mind rips them to shreds. "You idiot," I scream in my head. "Can't you spell?" People always compliment me on my great patience but I have no choice if I want to communicate.

I sometimes think that people are lucky that I can't talk. In Rehab I used to think the meanest thoughts about people, especially certain nurses. Someone would be staring at my face while feeding me and I'd be thinking "You are the stupidest person I've ever seen" or "You are such a twit." I don't remember always thinking such cruel and immature thoughts. I think it is a new behaviour. One of my nurses says it is just post-stroke anger being released.

Having a devastating stroke and living in a hospital for so long did not, I think, make me wiser. It did, however, render me totally neurotic. When I took ParaTranspo I would not ride up front for fear of being hurt in a head-on collision. I take aspirin every day to prevent another stroke. I insist on having the bathroom door shut at all times for fear that a small animal will come up the drain and bite my face. I know that some of my behaviour is crazy but it's hard to change.

At the moment I fear nearly everything because I'm locked in. I hope eventually to not be this way. I don't know if I need some kind of assistance to overcome my dumb fears or if I'm behaving normally for someone in my situation.

My father says my fears are quite normal. He says that if he couldn't move he'd be scared of everything too. I still find my behaviour embarrassing and disgusting. For a long time, I wouldn't go to visit any of my friends in my new van because I'm afraid of highway driving. Actually, I wouldn't even let my nurses drive on the main expressway here in Ottawa. I let my father drive because he is an ultra-cautious driver and almost as obsessed with safety as I am. My mother is a terrible driver, so I don't let her drive me anywhere. For a while, I didn't want them to travel in the same car in case there was an accident.

Eventually, I conquered my fear of driving on the highways. In August of 1993 I went in my van to visit Susan in Baltimore. The visit proved to be quite exhilarating and encouraging for my family and me.

Susan has now lived with locked-in syndrome for thirteen years. She can now walk with a walker. She can feed herself. On some days she can talk a bit. She even has a full-time job. Like me, she has tremendous support from her family and friends.

I don't know if Susan is an accurate predictor for me. I guess I'll have to wait and see.

❖

People expect this miserable experience to have enabled me to reach some deep philosophical conclusions about religion and God. In truth, I haven't reached any. I believe in God, but am no more or less religious than ever. I have, however, decided that people are inherently good. Since my stroke, I've met only very kind people. (With the exception of the low-life individual who recently stole my customized van — though of course I didn't really meet him or her.) I would think that my condition would invite the cruelest of comments and the most animated of laughs. But, to the contrary, I receive courteous treatment from everybody I encounter. I can't explain all the evil in the world, but I do think that people are innately kind.

I feel that I am surrounded by loving people — the best parents in the world and friends who show their love for me. I am not sure why I feel as happy as I do, but this has been true for some time — for years. Since the stroke, the only time I have not been happy was when I was in Rehab and was constantly afraid that I was going to be sent to the chronic-care hospital. I was afraid that steps were being taken to move in that direction and this troubled me greatly.

I recognize that my condition is not an encouraging one from the point of view of doctors. They do not offer any favorable prognosis but I also know that they are not in a position to judge what will happen in the future. I myself am optimistic but also realistic. I know that no one can give me assurances of what will happen in the future, but I face it with confidence and even faith. My faith is only partly from religious beliefs because I do not spend much time thinking about religion though I do believe in God. I don't read the Bible at this time, though I think it might be interesting for someone to read it to me.

❖

What I do know is that I am looking forward to a life where I can make a contribution in my own way. I continue to take courses —

I have even gone back to work on the statistics course I was taking when I had the stroke — and am determined to finish my undergraduate degree. I am confident that I have things to contribute and I want to do everything possible to get myself into a position where I can make that contribution. After I get my degree from Cornell I would like to go on and do graduate work — although no longer at Stanford as I originally thought. I'd eventually like to work in the field of psychology, but at this point, the sad reality is that there is no job that I am qualified to do. I correspond with other locked-in people in North America — all six of us. At least I am not completely alone.

But no matter what my future holds, I am happy and know that I can have a fulfilling and successful life.

Before my stroke, I was a normal teenager. I studied ballet and piano and always did well in school. I also sunbathed topless and stayed out all night.

Now there is just one girl. She is a determined girl. She can't move and she can't speak. She had a massive brain-stem stroke and she has written this book because she is determined that this should not happen to anyone else.

I still feel the same as I did before my stroke. I still have the same friends. I still have the same family. I still wear the same clothes. I still listen to the same radio station. I really haven't changed. This stroke may have damaged my motor abilities, but my personality isn't at all different. Just ask my friends and family. They know.

❖

Danielle: Especially in Rehab, Judy was able to respond to constant interruptions and invasion of privacy — tours of medical students and doctors, some of whom had no idea what was wrong with Judy or that she couldn't talk, would wander through the room, expecting one or the other of us to explain her medical condition — with great humour. During these invasions of her privacy, Judy would laugh at everything I said, making the medical students think she was coughing or gagging, and she would spell things like, "Are any of the guys cute?" while they were all still in the room.

Once Judy had moved to her apartment, I became a repository of Rehab horror stories. I tried always to have a wild story on hand for Judy's amusement and her friends' amazement. Judy had always maintained an appreciation of the absurdity of her position in Rehab, but I myself was astonished at how quickly her anger and bitterness faded in her new, more comfortable surroundings.

I really think Judy is an extraordinary woman. She is a sensitive, strong-willed, brilliant, irritating, wonderfully brave person. There is nothing I don't feel comfortable telling her. She is just like anyone else, and she is like no one else in the world. I'm so glad I met her, conquered my discomfort and got to know her, and can count on her as my friend.

Judy's grandparents: Judy is our oldest grandchild, and we had a close relationship with her as the child became the woman. A one-word description of Judy would have been vivacity — she was vivacious in all she did and had a buoyancy and spriteliness that were captivating and infectious. At the same time, whatever she undertook, she did so with real commitment. She was an excellent student and took responsibility seriously. When she talked about what she wanted to do with her life, it was in bubbly terms with the excitement of a young woman eager to discover the world for herself. When she was studying ballet, she was determined to become a fine dancer. When she spoke of wanting to be a psychologist, we had no doubt that she would be a good one, since she had a deep interest in people and enjoyed giving advice to her peers. In fact, we had the sense that Judy could accomplish anything she really wanted to do.

As Judy went through her months in the hospital and in Rehab, it became clear that there would not be a fast recovery from the stroke. But we were all grateful for one undeniable fact: Despite the predictions of doctors, she did not suffer a depression and early began to show upbeat spirit. She spoke of taking courses at Cornell so she could graduate with her class if possible. She talked of going into an apartment after she left Rehab so she could live an independent life. During our various trips to Ottawa, we saw painfully slow changes in her condition which she always told us about with excitement, revealing her confidence that things were moving in the right direction, however slowly.

Somehow Judy has maintained her sense of humour — even about her own stroke. On one visit, when we urged her to write poetry as she had done before the stroke, she suddenly blinked out, "I lie in my bed/Where I am washed, dressed, and fed/While nurses laugh above my head." We don't understand where she gets her strength or her spiritual inspiration, and how she manages to keep herself in such form even while she knows that her stroke has been a very serious one, and that she will have to endure a stiff, persistent, *unrelenting climb to make progress. We always leave her with a sense of optimism that she will yet overcome all which she is now enduring.*

Judy's parents: Judy was just the most magical kid. She has always been rather intense, focussed, determined. She would set her mind on things and then just work to make them happen. She was pretty realistic about her goals and had very high standards for herself. She was a talker — she would talk with her friends for hours and she always wanted to discuss everything with us. She was and is very dramatic, with a high energy level. She loves people and socializing with her friends has always been important. She was very caring and nurturing and took her friends' problems as a challenge to be solved. She was especially good at this and at giving advice. She did the same for us and for her brother — she had a way of taking us in hand and giving us suggestions. She and her brother got along fabulously and were very close and loving with each other. David idolized his older sister and was immensely proud of her. Judy, in turn, adored David and gave him tons of advice.

Judy was very patient and understanding with people she liked and very impatient and frustrated by those who irritated and or disappointed her. If something was important to her, she'd always persevere, but if she decided it wasn't worth her while, she'd let frustration creep in. We never would have said she was a patient person — she was too intense. However, since her stroke we have all learned to be patient. It's amazing how one can adjust one's sights and be pleased with small improvements and let nature set the pace.

The old physical Judy disappeared with the stroke, but the essential Judy did not. We have a vast collection of cards and poems that Judy made for us to celebrate birthdays, anniversaries, and holidays, and that stack has continued to grow since the stroke, as Judy blinks out her greetings and verses, the latter usually with an inventive rhyme scheme that features the word "stroke." Judy was and is very funny. She has a great sense of humour, much of it snappy and sarcastic. One of her major frustrations now is that having to spell out a funny punch line often causes it to lose most of its punch. Nevertheless, she still makes very funny comments and observations. Judy was and is a people person. And she continues to be concerned about the lives of her friends; when her nurses or her friends relate their problems and difficulties to Judy, she's always interested, and she usually has some advice.

Judy's brother: I think Judy's as happy as she ever was. The main reason it's been easier for me for the last few years is Judy's general attitude.

Judy has got to be the happiest quadriplegic on the face of this earth. I don't understand what it is that amuses Judy so much about life, but she's just one laugh after another. That's the real reason I'm dealing with this so well — it's really hard to get depressed when the person whose circumstances are depressing you is so happy.

SIXTEEN

"This stroke changed my life, but it didn't ruin it."

PEOPLE always feel sorry for me when I go out. They always think I was in a car accident.

A most bizarre thing happened to me recently. I was at the mall with my nurse when a middle-aged man gave her a bouquet of flowers for me. I had a mixed reaction to this. I love flowers and am always flattered to receive them. At the same time, I was a bit insulted. Did I look so pathetic that even a total stranger felt compelled to buy me flowers? That man didn't even know that I can't talk or feed myself. If he had, maybe he would have bought me the whole flower shop!

Once in a while an inquisitive being will ask my nurses what happened to me. They are never satisfied to learn that I had a stroke. One time when I was shopping with Andrea and my mother, a teenage girl saw me and turned to her mother. "Oh God, she can't talk," the girl exclaimed, "I feel so bad I want to cry." I caught sight of myself reflected in a mirror. "I can't believe this happened," I spelled to Andrea. "I can't believe I had a stroke."

"Karen, " I said to my nurse one morning, "Do you know why this stroke is so unbelievable?"

And I listed the reasons:

Because I was only nineteen. Nineteen-year-olds don't have strokes.

Because it was from the birth control pill. Everybody takes the pill—how could it be so dangerous?

Because I had to drop out of school and am finishing at Cornell by correspondence.

Because I can't move or talk. This stroke was absurd, leaving me able to understand everything, but unable to react.

Because I am not institutionalized.

Because I am content.

I am happy. I have everything I want and what I don't have I don't want.

❖

I really do find my stroke unbelievable.

❖

At present I have no long-term goals because I have no prognosis. One of my big goals was to avoid a chronic-care hospital, and now I am living in an apartment. I am still trying to get a call bell that really works. I am also hoping to use a computer to facilitate communication, but so far, nothing is faster than spelling with eye blinks. My first computer used a small video camera which was mounted on my wheelchair and took a picture of my eyes. It has a voice and says whatever I spell with my eyes. Unfortunately, using it is excruciatingly slow and difficult and frustrating. After an hour, both my nurse and I are drained, but I'm not giving up. I know Susan didn't like her computer at all when she first started either. This gives me hope and solace. I have been working with a better computer, but progress is very slow in this area.

My case is rare and unique and no neurologist in the world can tell me what my future will be. It is very frustrating not to know what to expect from life. I want to know if I'll ever walk, if I'll ever talk. Unfortunately, I was meant to not know. Yet I remain undaunted.

Appendices

AFTERWORD A

*Some Thoughts for Doctors, Nurses, and
Other Health Care Professionals*

IN the time since my stroke, I have had far greater and closer contact with doctors, nurses, therapists, and other members of the health-care profession than I could ever have imagined would be my fate.

I really liked most of my doctors. Dr. Nelson, for instance, was terrific. He had a thorough and likable bedside manner. He was patient and chatty. He never scolded me, for which I was tremendously grateful. One thing that bothers me about many people is that they are too intimidated to spell with me. They understand the basis of my communication system, but are reluctant to try it. When I was in the hospital, if neither of my parents was there to interpret, people simply asked questions that could be answered "yes" or "no." At first, Dr. Nelson didn't spell with me, but then, to his credit, he learned my system.

Dr. Grinnell too was very pleasant—very intelligent and extremely calm, even though I fit the textbook definition of a "bad patient." "Bad patients" demand a lot of time and attention; I certainly was guilty of that. I didn't get the kind of treatment I needed in the hospital, therefore I was demanding, rude, and manipulative in an attempt to get the amount of care I needed. I was a terrible patient, but Dr. Grinnell never chastised me for my behavior. She listened to me and took my concerns seriously.

Unfortunately, I didn't always have such good experiences with doctors. I had a fiasco with the Rehab podiatrist which culminated in one of my toe nails being ripped off without an anesthetic. Since my stroke I had been getting ingrown toe nails. I had had many encounters with the podiatrist and had several minor operations on my toe nails. One morning I was scheduled to have another minor toe operation. The podiatrist was going to remove a corner of the nail. Dr. Grinnell froze the small part of the toe that the podiatrist said he would cut. When he actually saw it, he decided to remove the entire nail — without freezing. My nurse Marilyn was with me, but she couldn't do anything. The procedure hurt so much that I sat up. I guess my muscles just remembered how to react and they wanted to show that podiatrist what I was feeling. Didn't he know I had full sensation and could feel everything? If I could have yanked my foot away and screamed, I would have.

I also hated intensely that the Rehabilitation Centre was part of a teaching hospital. Every morning a group of doctors and residents did rounds, which gave them a chance to gawk at my rare and extreme condition. I had no say in the matter. This morning parade of strangers was also a huge invasion of my privacy. Nor was it just in Rehab. When I went to the hospital with a mysterious hip infection recently, all of the doctors freaked out because they had never seen a person with locked-in syndrome before. It really disturbed me.

All in all, my experiences with doctors have been quite positive, but when they were negative, they were terrible. Little things, like taking the effort to learn my communication system, being patient and kind, and treating me with tact, dignity, and understanding meant a lot to me, and are essential to a good doctor-patient relationship.

❖

For the most part I got along famously with my various therapists, but I have terrible memories of one physiotherapist who sometimes helped with my sessions in Rehab. This physiotherapist had especially bad body odor. I was shocked and thought this highly inappropriate for a physiotherapist. I had always been extremely sensitive to smells and this just disgusted me.

❖

I don't think most nurses realize how important they are to certain patients. To very elderly and lonely patients, or very physically dependent patients, like myself, the nurse plays a central role. Nurses are even more important to many patients than doctors or therapists because nurses have prolonged intimate contact with their patients. I, for instance, rely upon my nurse to communicate with other people and even to eat.

This is my biggest pet peeve: nurses who don't know my care.

When I was in the hospital and in Rehab, I often had nurses who couldn't spell with me or take care of me properly. This was disastrous. I absolutely dreaded new nurses; their blunders were enormous. I had several catastrophes with new nurses.

One night, when I was still in Rehab, I got a migraine. This, of course, terrified me. I couldn't trigger the call bell so I had to wait until I was checked. Unfortunately, I was checked by two nurses who didn't know me. I batted my eyes, indicating that I wanted to spell. The nurses understood that but they didn't know how to spell. They thought I was being cute and funny! I lay awake with an unmedicated migraine until morning when a nurse who knew me finally arrived.

Another example: I need to swallow pills whole. I can't swallow them crushed up. One new nurse assumed that I needed my pills crushed up. She crushed them and shoved them down my throat. My coughing and gagging didn't deter her. I blinked my eyes wildly, but, of course, she didn't know that signal.

I feel that I am in a prime position to determine what makes a good nurse. Firstly, a good nurse can obviously communicate with the patient. This is basic and key. Even if the patient can't speak verbally, it is the nurse's responsibility to learn to communicate with that patient.

My communication system of spelling with eye blinks was a huge success with the regular Rehab staff. Most were quite adept at spelling with me. Some, like Marilyn, had even memorized my code. The relief staff, however, were terrible. They never could spell with me or feed me and didn't bother to learn. I would have thought a nurse responsible for me would want to know how I communicated. How wrong I was!

I hate nurses who cannot think for themselves but always must follow a planned routine or schedule. Marilyn was particularly sensitive to her patients and always made sure she knew what was going on with them. She took the trouble to learn my communication system and she didn't assume that she knew everything. One day I told Marilyn that despite the written warnings taped up around my bed, I wasn't allergic to chocolate. I told her that I'd been secretly eating it for years. I guess Marilyn believed me because she gave me a little bit. Nothing happened. From then on, I had chocolate regularly.

I also feel that the nurse should learn special needs and preferences of his or her patient. I hated that most nurses didn't know my special breakfast and didn't bother to look at my chart to learn what I eat. There were a few nurses, however, whom I could trust always to fix me the right breakfast.

At Rehab there were RNs — registered nurses — and RNAs — registered nursing assistants. An RNA is like an RN except she can't give medication. My favourite evening nurse was Karen. She was genuinely interested in all her patients. I simply loved her. She even sort of knew the names of my friends. She always asked me if my friends were visiting on the weekend and tried to guess who. She knew all about me.

My favourite RNA at Rehab was Natalie. She was just twenty-seven years old. She was one of the few Rehab nurses who actually had a lot in common with me. I could relate well to her. I was always glad and relieved when Natalie was on. Nat was rarely assigned to me but she always took care of me anyway.

❖

I am very picky about some things. I like my nurses to be young and female. They can relate better to me and they have greater enthusiasm for the job. I had various student nurses while I was in Rehab. I think someone tried to match me up in age with them. I really enjoyed having student nurses. Although it was frustrating at first when the students didn't know how to do anything, I eventually appreciated having someone my age to talk to.

Once I began to make plans to leave Rehab, I began hiring my own nurses. One personal nurse I have now told me that she became a nurse because she didn't like the way her grandmother was treated in the hospital. I know exactly what she means. I adore and cherish and appreciate my new independence. I had cried every day in the hospital. I never cry now that I am living in my own apartment. One reason I am so happy is because I have chosen the nurses who work with me.

I think that to truly empathize with a patient, a doctor or nurse or anyone who cares about the individual should try to endure what the patient must. Try to spend all night with your legs in one position without shifting; try to go to a restaurant and be fed; try being transferred from bed to chair: this is the only way to really appreciate what the patient experiences and feels. My mother has tried most of these things and nobody even suggested them to her. She was simply curious.

❖

I think caregivers should also try to put themselves in the patient's place. Although I have learned to become detached from whatever is being done to my body, I still need to be treated with respect and tact. I was very uncomfortable with male nurses dressing me and undressing me and providing my care, and I shouldn't have had to fight so hard to have female nurses. Supervisory staff should consider whether they would have been comfortable with this situation when they were my age.

AFTERWORD B

*Coping and Helping: Some Thoughts for
Friends and Family Members*

Coping

JUDY'S parents: A word on coping. People in our situation *have*
to cope. As friends and family came to see us and Judy, we often
saw written on their faces the true despair they were feeling. Although we were terrified and overwhelmed by the events that were
unfolding, we had no time to dwell on the true horror of the moment. That was something others had the luxury of doing. We had
to get from one minute and one day to the next. In a situation such
as ours, there was no time to really get in touch with our feelings
because we always had this situation waiting for us and Judy was
ever in need of our love, strength, and attention. We supported each
other, and at the same time, remarked that this would be completely
impossible for a single parent to endure.

People would always say, "You're so strong," and "I could never
cope the way you have," but actually, what was the alternative?
Faced with a catastrophe, you cope or die. We coped the best way
we could.

We felt that we were floundering in a world without guidelines.
We had no idea what was coming next, what to expect, and it was
terrifying. As parents, you always carry a mental list of the various
horrors that might afflict your children — car accidents, cancer or
other illnesses, etc. — but nowhere in your repertoire are you prepared for your child to have a stroke. We had no benchmark against
which to judge our situation.

One thing that helped for a while was our meeting with a support group for family members of stroke patients. The support group was organized by the social worker during the first months that Judy was in Rehab. We met once a week for about six weeks. There were usually from four to six people in addition to ourselves.

The other participants had husbands or wives or a parent who had had a stroke. We would go around the room, each person describing what it was like to deal with this new situation. Emotions ran high. People opened up about their feelings and about their difficulties in coping with their situations.

We were the only ones with a child who was a stroke patient. When we talked about Judy, the circumstances of her stroke, her locked-in condition, and the dim prospects for her recovery, it literally stopped the conversation. Judy's circumstances helped put everyone else's in a different perspective. Most of the others saw their own situations a little differently after we discussed Judy and her unpromising prognosis.

We found the group to be enormously helpful. It offered us a chance to talk at a time when we were feeling quite fragile. It also helped us feel more connected to other people whom we saw as daily visitors to Rehab, people involved in the same grinding regimen of visiting, trying to appear cheerful in front of their sick relatives when they were really in great despair. We found it helpful to compare notes about the feelings, coping mechanisms, and planning for transition out of Rehab — the steps toward leaving the hospital and the modifications that would be needed to adapt home or apartments.

Planning

During the period of waiting and hoping for Judy's release from Rehab into her own apartment, we also considered modifying our house and bringing Judy home to live with us. We talked about adding a new bedroom, living area, and bathroom that would accommodate Judy and a nurse/attendant. We obtained the names of architects and designers who were experienced with wheelchair accessible design. We actually did widen our front door and replace our front step with a sloped entry way. We believed that it would be much better for Judy to live at home, out of an institution, but we were also motivated by the hope that having her home would ease our routine of running to the hospital every day. We were on a treadmill, trying to balance work, home, and David with the demands of being with Judy.

It is likely that, had Judy come home to live, the demands on us would have remained almost as great, minus the running to the hospital. It is also likely that Judy would not have developed the same sense of independence that she has living in her own apartment.

How Friends and Family Members Can Help

One cannot survive an event of this magnitude without the support of family and friends. Although this need is most urgent in the beginning, when everyone is most concerned and eager to do something to help, friends should not hesitate to get involved later on. In a long-term situation, the family may need more, not less, assistance as time passes, and offers of help are always appreciated.

At first we were so overwhelmed by Judy's medical crisis that we weren't able to avail ourselves of all the offers of assistance we received. However, after several months, and years, when we knew more about our and Judy's needs, we knew better how to direct and utilize offers of assistance.

It is natural for people to want to help friends going through a crisis. But what to do? At first we were inundated with cards, letters, and calls. This generous show of concern was helpful as a show of support.

As we had so little time and energy left over at the end of the day, we knew we could not cope with the phone calls; thus, we were fortunate to have Ken's brother Dan and his wife Joy in Ottawa to answer many calls and questions. Once we returned to Ottawa from Ithaca, we installed a telephone answering machine at home. We left updated messages on the tape so friends would know what was happening with Judy. And when we came home at the end of long days at the hospital, comforting messages were waiting for us.

Another great source of comfort was the food and meals provided by family and friends. It was difficult for us to rush home from the hospital or work, fix a meal, and rush back to the hospital to be with Judy, but we couldn't conceive of doing anything else. Dan and Joy lived a ten-minute walk from the hospital. Almost every night that first summer, we went there for dinner. The break was a Godsend and really kept us alive. After dinner we would walk back to the hospital. Often, meals were dropped off at Joy's by friends who knew how important it was for us to eat well and avoid getting sick; they provided us with baked goods, casseroles, and salads. These were invaluable.

Food is very basic, but it was something everyone could help with and it was greatly appreciated. This assistance with meals gave us an alternative to eating yet another meal in the hospital cafeteria. One set of friends not only thought of our needs, but as Judy began to eat more and more real food, prepared special dishes for her as well.

Besides providing meals, the area in which friends were most helpful was in visiting Judy in the hospital or Rehab. We were haunted by the knowledge that if no one was visiting Judy, she would probably be lying in her room, alone and lonely. Knowing that Judy had a visitor gave us the option of changing our routine and spending an evening at home.

An offer from a friend is much easier on the family than having to ask someone to visit. However, we did call on friends outright and ask them to help on the rare occasions we arranged to get away for a few days for a break. Before leaving, we would arrange a schedule of visitors so that Judy had lots of company in our absence. In order to avoid putting too great a burden on anyone in particular, the visiting days were divided up and the visiting shared by friends and family. Although Judy often felt insecure when we were away, we believe she enjoyed the varied social life offered by many visitors as a substitute for the steady diet of mom and dad.

After Judy's stroke, some friends dropped out of our lives completely and others seemed to drop in to stay. Our dear friend Jane took on herself the task of feeding Judy lunch on Tuesdays and Thursdays while she was in Rehab, which meant that there were two days a week Anne could have lunch with friends at work. She did this for over a year and a half. There is no way we can ever repay her for her kindness and support.

Our employers were wonderful, telling us both to take as much time off as we needed. That first summer, Anne was off work until Labor Day. Then, for the next year or so, her office paid her by the hour instead of an annual salary. That way, she never felt she was letting anyone down if she needed to spend more time with Judy and her employers wouldn't feel they weren't getting as much from her as they would like. The people at Ken's office were also very generous and understanding. Ken was granted some leave during the summer, and when he returned to work there was sufficient flexibility to accommodate the rigorous demands of Judy's stroke. Our attention was usually with Judy and we would have been hopeless at work with our usual job expectations. Even now, neither one of us is able to concentrate in quite the same way we used to before the stroke.

❖

Judy's grandparents: When Anne and Ken called us from Ithaca and told us that Judy was hospitalized with an undiagnosed illness, we immediately flew to Ithaca. We stayed for about five days, spending endless hours in the hospital and waiting for some comforting word that the situation was improving. When Judy was moved back to Ottawa for hospitalization, we went back to Washington, D.C. but kept in touch with Anne and Ken over the weeks and months that followed, phoning regularly and visiting often.

We recognized in the early weeks that an important part of our visits to Ottawa was to support Anne and Ken as they went through this agonizing experience and to try to be helpful to them in any way we could. We were there not only as parents but as friends with whom they could share their feelings, and we have been gratified that our relationship with them has grown closer than ever because of what we have shared together. It has been moving to see the relationship between Ken and Anne grow ever closer since Judy's stroke as they have had to modify their way of life drastically in order to be able to devote themselves so fully to Judy, and at the same time give David their care and attention.

Networking

Judy's grandparents: One of the first things we did after Judy had her stroke was to try to gather as much information as possible on strokes, particularly those affecting the brain stem, in the hope that this might offer some useful guidance in dealing with her condition and her future.

Judy's grandfather took it upon himself to try to find experts knowledgeable about "locked-in syndrome" and made arrangements for Dr. Fred Plum, who had coined the term and was an expert in the field, to see Judy. He was also in touch with Dr. Richard Johnson, head of Neurology at the Johns Hopkins Medical School, Dean Tosteson, Dean of the Medical School at Harvard, and other physicians with whom he came into contact and who had some familiarity with the condition. He called physicians and scientists at the Weizmann Institute in Israel who were working on some aspects of the problems, arranged for library and computer searches through the University of Maryland and the National Institutes of Health (NIH), and contacted other people at a number of institutions, both in the U.S. and abroad, in each case inquiring as to whether there might be central registry where we could get information about Judy's condition, especially about the experience other people might have had with the problem.

We were able to pick up bits and pieces here and there but nowhere was there a central repository of relevant information. We originally learned about Susan, the young woman who has become something of a role model to Judy, through a reference in an article in an engineering journal. Although Susan lives in Baltimore and her computer had been designed for her by a man working in the Applied Physics Laboratory at Johns Hopkins, no one at the Johns Hopkins Medical School seemed aware of her existence. The staff there got in touch with her father only after we reported where and how she could be reached.

Admittedly, Judy's case is rare and it probably should not be surprising that there is not much information about how others deal with her situation. But our experience at the very least suggests that considered efforts should be made to set up some kind of central clearing house either at NIH or elsewhere where all such relevant data can be brought together and recorded. Several months ago we learned that efforts are beings made by the American Stroke Association to deal with the problem.

APPENDIX

What Everyone Should Know About Stroke

Facts on Stroke

- Stroke afflicts over half a million people each year in Canada and the U.S.
- Stroke kills over 150,000 people each year and disables another 200,000.
- Stroke is the third leading cause of death in Canada and the U.S., and the number one cause of adult disability.
- Although the risk of stroke rises with age, a stroke can happen at any age.

Signs and Symptoms of Stroke

- Sudden numbness, weakness, or paralysis of face, arm, or leg — especially on one side of the body.
- Temporary dizziness, loss of balance or coordination, or an unexplained fall.
- Sudden blurred or decreased vision in one or both eyes.
- Difficulty in speaking or understanding simple statements.
- An episode of double vision.

If you experience any of these symptoms, alone or in combination, for a short period of time (a few minutes to a few hours), you may be experiencing a transient ischemic attack (TIA), or mini-stroke and should see a doctor promptly.

Risk Factors for Strokes

- Two-thirds of all strokes happen to people over the age of 65.
- More men than women have strokes, but because women tend to live longer than men, most stroke survivors over the age of 65 are women.
- In North America, African-Americans have a higher risk of stroke than any other racial group.
- Anyone with a family history of stroke or transient ischemic attacks (TIA) is at greater than average risk for stroke.
- Anyone who has a personal history of diabetes is at greater than average risk for stroke.
- Having high blood pressure (hypertension) puts people at higher risk of stroke; between 40% and 70% of all stroke patients had high blood pressure before the stroke.
- Having high cholesterol levels puts people at greater risk for stroke.
- Having a personal history of heart disease increases the risk of stroke; heart disease makes a person six times more likely to have a stroke.
- Sufferers of one or more strokes or TIAs are at increased risk for having another.
- Smoking increases the risk of stroke; this is especially the case for women over age 30 who take birth control pills. These women are 22 times more likely to have a stroke.
- Heavy drinking puts the drinker at increased risk of stroke.
- Being overweight increases the risk of stroke.

Resources

Heart and Stroke Association of Canada
160 George Street, Suite 200
Ottawa, Ontario
CANADA K1N 9M2
(613) 523-9357

National Stroke Association
8480 East Orchard Road, Suite 1000
Englewood, Colorado
USA 80111-5015
(313) 771-1700

American Heart Association/Stroke Connection
7272 Greenville Avenue
Dallas, Texas USA 75231-4596
(800) 553-6321 (Monday–Friday, 8:30 a.m.–5:00 p.m. CST)

The Golden Dog Press

This volume was produced using the TEX typesetting system, with Adobe Palatino POSTSCRIPT fonts.